CONTENTS

INTRODUCTION 6

How Does an Air Fryer Work? 6

HOW TO USE AN AIR FRYER 8

Five Tips for Using an Air Fryer 8

FISH AND SEAFOOD RECIPES 9

Crabmeat-stuffed Flounder 9

Fish Sticks For Kids 10

Crispy Smelts 11

Lemon-dill Salmon Burgers 12

Shrimp 13

Fish Sticks With Tartar Sauce 14

Catfish Nuggets 15

Potato-wrapped Salmon Fillets 16

Nutty Shrimp With Amaretto Glaze 17

Coconut Jerk Shrimp 18

Fish-in-chips 19

SANDWICHES AND BURGERS RECIPES 20

Sausage And Pepper Heros 20

Chicken Gyros 21

Chicken Club Sandwiches 22

Chicken Spiedies 23

Asian Glazed Meatballs 24

Reuben Sandwiches 25

White Bean Veggie Burgers 26

Chicken Saltimbocca Sandwiches 27

Salmon Burgers 28

Turkey Burgers 29

Thai-style Pork Sliders 30

VEGETARIANS RECIPES 31

Charred Cauliflower Tacos 31

Egg Rolls 32

Quinoa Burgers With Feta Cheese And Dill....................................33

Cheese Ravioli 35

Falafel 36

Veggie Fried Rice 37

Broccoli Cheddar Stuffed Potatoes...38

Parmesan Portobello Mushroom Caps 39

Tacos 40

Vegetable Hand Pies...41

Mexican Twice Air-fried Sweet Potatoes 42

DESSERTS AND SWEETS 43

Chocolate Macaroons 43

Fudgy Brownie Cake 44

Coconut Crusted Bananas With Pineapple Sauce 45

Mixed Berry Hand Pies 46

Blueberry Crisp...47

Fried Snickers Bars 48

Easy Churros 49

Giant Oatmeal–peanut Butter Cookie...50

Coconut-custard Pie 51

Fried Cannoli Wontons..52

Nutella® Torte 53

BREAD AND BREAKFAST 54

Spinach And Artichoke White Pizza..54

Egg And Sausage Crescent Rolls 55

Blueberry Muffins..56

Bacon Puff Pastry Pinwheels 57

Ham And Cheddar Gritters 58

Southwest Cornbread 59

Fry Bread 60

Cheddar-ham-corn Muffins 61

Sweet Potato-cinnamon Toast 62

Peppered Maple Bacon Knots 63

Crustless Broccoli, Roasted Pepper And Fontina Quiche 64

VEGETABLE SIDE DISHES RECIPES 65

Bacon-wrapped Asparagus...65

Street Corn 66

Roasted Eggplant Halves With Herbed Ricotta 67

Moroccan-spiced Carrots..68

Panzanella Salad With Crispy Croutons..69

Green Peas With Mint 70

Green Beans 71

Steak Fries 72

Five-spice Roasted Sweet Potatoes 73

Stuffed Avocados..74

BEEF , PORK & LAMB RECIPES 75

Steakhouse Burgers With Red Onion Compote...75

Perfect Strip Steaks 76

Barbecue-style Beef Cube Steak 77

Sweet And Sour Pork 78

Meat Loaves 80

Lamb Chops 81

Sausage-cheese Calzone...82

Crunchy Fried Pork Loin Chops 84

Pork Schnitzel With Dill Sauce...85

Chicken-fried Steak..87

APPETIZERS AND SNACKS 88

    Cheese Straws 88

    Zucchini Fries With Roasted Garlic Aïoli 89

    Spicy Sweet Potato Tater-tots 90

    Thick-crust Pepperoni Pizza 91

    Polenta Fries With Chili-lime Mayo 92

    Herbed Cheese Brittle 93

    Onion Puffs 94

    Potato Chips 95

    String Bean Fries 96

    Fried Olives 97

POULTRY RECIPES 98

    Chicken Parmesan 98

    Chicken Wellington 99

    Teriyaki Chicken Legs 101

    Simple Buttermilk Fried Chicken 102

    Fiesta Chicken Plate 103

    Air-fried Turkey Breast With Cherry Glaze 104

    Sesame Orange Chicken 105

    Crispy "fried" Chicken 106

    Southern-fried Chicken Livers 107

    Spicy Black Bean Turkey Burgers With Cumin-avocado Spread 108

RECIPES INDEX 110

INTRODUCTION

How Does an Air Fryer Work?

The first think you're probably wondering is how an Air Fryer works. How is it any different than a regular deep fryer or an oven? Most importantly, Air Fryers are different from regular deep fryers because they don't actually fry food, meaning you don't actually submerge your food in hot oil to cook it.

The actual mechanism of Air Fryers is most akin to that of a convection oven. Basically, your food is placed in a perforated metal basket. At the top is a heating unit with a high powered fan that blows the hot air all around the food, creating a convection effect that nicely and evenly browns the outside of the food. And unlike a convection oven, Air Fryers are compact, allowing for faster and more efficient preheating and cooking times.

10 Reasons to Buy an Air Fryer

1) It makes delicious food !

When you bake food in regular ovens (especially not convention ovens), you are often left with uneven results, with some parts burnt and other parts undercooked. The mechanism of Air Fryers described above allows hot air to circulate all around the food, maximizing surface area-to-heat ratio and allowing for perfectly even crispiness and crunchiness. While an Air Fryer won't taste exactly like if you used a traditional deep fryer, we really love the end result of each recipe we've tried so far.

2) It is a healthier option

Love the taste of fried food but not the way it makes you feel afterwards (for instance Zoe tends to get heartburn with fried food)? Are you disappointed with the end result when you try the oven-roasted version of the same recipe? If yes to these questions, then an Air Fryer might be the solution!

You can usually get away with using little-to-no oil when cooking with an Air Fryer, which can cut calories. Furthermore, one study (Sansano et at., 2015) showed that compared to traditional frying methods, using an air fryer reduces acrylamide (a compound associated with certain types of cancer) by up to 90%.

3) It is time and energy efficient

With their compact size and efficient circulation of hot air, Air Fryers out-compete your oven. With most recipes only needing 8-20 minutes of cooking, Air Fryers reduce cooking time by up to 25% (they also only need a fraction of the time to preheat, unlike your oven), saving you both time and energy.

4) There's an air fryer for every price range

With prices as low as $40, buying an Air Fryer doesn't have to break your wallet. We are obviously more than happy with our investment in an Air Fryer. And don't worry, even the lower-priced ones still produce great results! Keep reading this Ultimate Air Fryer Guide to see the specific products we recommend.

5) They are easy to clean

With removable parts, nonstick materials, and most being dishwasher-safe, cleaning your air fryer is no hassle at all! And compared to the grease that coats your kitchen walls after deep frying foods, an Air Fryer produces no mess.

6) They are versatile and can make all kinds of recipes

See below for a sample of all of the different types of food you can make using an Air Fryer. From meat to vegetables to even pizza, we've been able to incorporate air frying into a ton of our meal preparations.

7) Many have different modes, allowing different types of cooking

Not only used for frying foods, an Air Fryer can also be used for reheating leftovers, thawing frozen food, and much, much more. Ours lets you change the settings to "air fry", "roast", "dehydrate", and "reheat". It's up to you to experiment!

8) They come in all different shapes and sizes

It's true that they take up some counter space. But there's an Air Fryer of every size to fit your needs. If you mostly cook for one or two people, you can get away with 2 to 3 quart sized Air Fryers. If you usually cook for a family of 3-5, consider 5 to 6 quart ones. But generally, air fryers between 3 to 5 quarts are versatile enough for most types and quantities of cooking.

9) They make for a great gift

What a perfect gift for the budding home chef?! I got ours for Zoe for Christmas. But whether its for a birthday, wedding registry, or any other special occasion, an Air Fryer makes for an ideal long-lasting and useful present.

10) They let you join the Air Fryer community

With niche Air Fryer blogs to Air Fryer recipe books, buying one of these lets you drastically expand your culinary repertoire and connect with a whole new community of home chefs.

HOW TO USE AN AIR FRYER

The Air Fryer's Versatility

Get ready to challenge everything you know about frying foods. Air fryers can fry your favorite foods to crispy, golden brown perfection (yes, French fries and potato chips!) using little or no oil. Not only can you make traditionally fried foods like potato chips and French fries, but it's also great for vegetables, proteins like chicken wings and drummettes, and appetizers like coquettes and feta triangles. Even desserts like brownies and blondies are perfectly baked in an air fryer.

Why It Works

Put in other terms, an air fryer is much like a convection oven but in a different outfit, cooking food at very high temperatures while simultaneously circulating dry air around the food, cooking food faster all the while making it crisp without needing to add extra fat.

Five Tips for Using an Air Fryer

1. Shake it.

Be sure to open the air fryer and shake foods around as they "fry" in the machine's basket—smaller foods like French fries and chips can compress. For best results, rotate them every 5-10 minutes.

2. Don't overcrowd.

Give foods plenty of space so that the air can circulate effectively; that's what gives you crispy results. Our test kitchen cooks swear by the air fryer for snacks and small batches.

3. Give foods a spray.

Lightly spray foods with cooking spray or add just a bit of oil to ensure they don't stick to the basket.

4. Keep it dry.

Pat foods dry before cooking (if they are marinated, for example) to avoid splattering and excess smoke. Similarly, when cooking high-fat foods like chicken wings, make sure to empty the fat from the bottom machine periodically.

5. Master other cooking methods.

The air fryer isn't just for frying; it's great for other healthy cooking methods like baking, roasting and grilling, too. Our test kitchen also loves to use the machine for cooking salmon!

FISH AND SEAFOOD RECIPES

Crabmeat-stuffed Flounder

Servings:3
Cooking Time: 12 Minutes

Ingredients:

- 4½ ounces Purchased backfin or claw crabmeat, picked over for bits of shell and cartilage
- 6 Saltine crackers, crushed into fine crumbs
- 2 tablespoons plus 1 teaspoon Regular or low-fat mayonnaise (not fat-free)
- ¾ teaspoon Yellow prepared mustard
- 1½ teaspoons Worcestershire sauce
- ⅛ teaspoon Celery salt
- 3 5- to 6-ounce skinless flounder fillets
- Vegetable oil spray
- Mild paprika

Directions:

1. Preheat the air fryer to 400°F.
2. Gently mix the crabmeat, crushed saltines, mayonnaise, mustard, Worcestershire sauce, and celery salt in a bowl until well combined.
3. Generously coat the flat side of a fillet with vegetable oil spray. Set the fillet sprayed side down on your work surface. Cut the fillet in half widthwise, then cut one of the halves in half lengthwise. Set a scant ⅓ cup of the crabmeat mixture on top of the undivided half of the fish fillet, mounding the mixture to make an oval that somewhat fits the shape of the fillet with at least a ¼-inch border of fillet beyond the filling all around.
4. Take the two thin divided quarters (that is, the halves of the half) and lay them lengthwise over the filling, overlapping at each end and leaving a little space in the middle where the filling peeks through. Coat the top of the stuffed flounder piece with vegetable oil spray, then sprinkle paprika over the stuffed flounder fillet. Set aside and use the remaining fillet(s) to make more stuffed flounder "packets," repeating steps 3 and
5. Use a nonstick-safe spatula to transfer the stuffed flounder fillets to the basket. Leave as much space between them as possible. Air-fry undisturbed for 12 minutes, or until lightly brown and firm (but not hard).
6. Use that same spatula, plus perhaps another one, to transfer the fillets to a serving platter or plates. Cool for a minute or two, then serve hot.

Fish Sticks For Kids

Servings: 8
Cooking Time: 6 Minutes

Ingredients:
- 8 ounces fish fillets (pollock or cod)
- salt (optional)
- ½ cup plain breadcrumbs
- oil for misting or cooking spray

Directions:
1. Cut fish fillets into "fingers" about ½ x 3 inches. Sprinkle with salt to taste, if desired.
2. Roll fish in breadcrumbs. Spray all sides with oil or cooking spray.
3. Place in air fryer basket in single layer and cook at 390°F for 6 minutes, until golden brown and crispy.

Crispy Smelts

Servings:3

Cooking Time: 20 Minutes

Ingredients:

- 1 pound Cleaned smelts
- 3 tablespoons Tapioca flour
- Vegetable oil spray
- To taste Coarse sea salt or kosher salt

Directions:

1. Preheat the air fryer to 400°F.
2. Toss the smelts and tapioca flour in a large bowl until the little fish are evenly coated.
3. Lay the smelts out on a large cutting board. Lightly coat both sides of each fish with vegetable oil spray.
4. When the machine is at temperature, set the smelts close together in the basket, with a few even overlapping on top. Air-fry undisturbed for 20 minutes, until lightly browned and crisp.
5. Remove the basket from the machine and turn out the fish onto a wire rack. The smelts will most likely come out as one large block, or maybe in a couple of large pieces. Cool for a minute or two, then sprinkle the smelts with salt and break the block(s) into much smaller sections or individual fish to serve.

Lemon-dill Salmon Burgers

Servings: 4
Cooking Time: 8 Minutes

Ingredients:

- 2 (6-ounce) fillets of salmon, finely chopped by hand or in a food processor
- 1 cup fine breadcrumbs
- 1 teaspoon freshly grated lemon zest
- 2 tablespoons chopped fresh dill weed
- 1 teaspoon salt
- freshly ground black pepper
- 2 eggs, lightly beaten
- 4 brioche or hamburger buns
- lettuce, tomato, red onion, avocado, mayonnaise or mustard, to serve

Directions:

1. Preheat the air fryer to 400°F.
2. Combine all the ingredients in a bowl. Mix together well and divide into four balls. Flatten the balls into patties, making an indentation in the center of each patty with your thumb (this will help the burger stay flat as it cooks) and flattening the sides of the burgers so that they fit nicely into the air fryer basket.
3. Transfer the burgers to the air fryer basket and air-fry for 4 minutes. Flip the burgers over and air-fry for another 3 to 4 minutes, until nicely browned and firm to the touch.
4. Serve on soft brioche buns with your choice of topping – lettuce, tomato, red onion, avocado, mayonnaise or mustard.

Shrimp

Servings: 4
Cooking Time: 8 Minutes

Ingredients:

- 1 pound (26–30 count) shrimp, peeled, deveined, and butterflied (last tail section of shell intact)
- Marinade
- 1 5-ounce can evaporated milk
- 2 eggs, beaten
- 2 tablespoons white vinegar
- 1 tablespoon baking powder
- Coating
- 1 cup crushed panko breadcrumbs
- ½ teaspoon paprika
- ½ teaspoon Old Bay Seasoning
- ¼ teaspoon garlic powder
- oil for misting or cooking spray

Directions:

1. Stir together all marinade ingredients until well mixed. Add shrimp and stir to coat. Refrigerate for 1 hour.
2. When ready to cook, preheat air fryer to 390°F.
3. Combine coating ingredients in shallow dish.
4. Remove shrimp from marinade, roll in crumb mixture, and spray with olive oil or cooking spray.
5. Cooking in two batches, place shrimp in air fryer basket in single layer, close but not overlapping. Cook at 390°F for 8 minutes, until light golden brown and crispy.
6. Repeat step 5 to cook remaining shrimp.

Fish Sticks With Tartar Sauce

Servings: 2

Cooking Time: 6 Minutes

Ingredients:

- 12 ounces cod or flounder
- ½ cup flour
- ½ teaspoon paprika
- 1 teaspoon salt
- lots of freshly ground black pepper
- 2 eggs, lightly beaten
- 1½ cups panko breadcrumbs
- 1 teaspoon salt
- vegetable oil
- Tartar Sauce:
- ¼ cup mayonnaise
- 2 teaspoons lemon juice
- 2 tablespoons finely chopped sweet pickles
- salt and freshly ground black pepper

Directions:

1. Cut the fish into ¾-inch wide sticks or strips. Set up a dredging station. Combine the flour, paprika, salt and pepper in a shallow dish. Beat the eggs lightly in a second shallow dish. Finally, mix the breadcrumbs and salt in a third shallow dish. Coat the fish sticks by dipping the fish into the flour, then the egg and finally the breadcrumbs, coating on all sides in each step and pressing the crumbs firmly onto the fish. Place the finished sticks on a plate or baking sheet while you finish all the sticks.
2. Preheat the air fryer to 400°F.
3. Spray the fish sticks with the oil and spray or brush the bottom of the air fryer basket. Place the fish into the basket and air-fry at 400°F for 4 minutes, turn the fish sticks over, and air-fry for another 2 minutes.
4. While the fish is cooking, mix the tartar sauce ingredients together.
5. Serve the fish sticks warm with the tartar sauce and some French fries on the side.

Catfish Nuggets

Servings: 4
Cooking Time: 7 Minutes Per Batch

Ingredients:
- 2 medium catfish fillets, cut in chunks (approximately 1 x 2 inch)
- salt and pepper
- 2 eggs
- 2 tablespoons skim milk
- ½ cup cornstarch
- 1 cup panko breadcrumbs, crushed
- oil for misting or cooking spray

Directions:
1. Season catfish chunks with salt and pepper to your liking.
2. Beat together eggs and milk in a small bowl.
3. Place cornstarch in a second small bowl.
4. Place breadcrumbs in a third small bowl.
5. Dip catfish chunks in cornstarch, dip in egg wash, shake off excess, then roll in breadcrumbs.
6. Spray all sides of catfish chunks with oil or cooking spray.
7. Place chunks in air fryer basket in a single layer, leaving space between for air circulation.
8. Cook at 390°F for 4minutes, turn, and cook an additional 3 minutes, until fish flakes easily and outside is crispy brown.
9. Repeat steps 7 and 8 to cook remaining catfish nuggets.

Potato-wrapped Salmon Fillets

Servings:3
Cooking Time: 8 Minutes

Ingredients:

- 1 Large 1-pound elongated yellow potato(es), peeled
- 3 6-ounce, 1½-inch-wide, quite thick skinless salmon fillets
- Olive oil spray
- ¼ teaspoon Table salt
- ¼ teaspoon Ground black pepper

Directions:

1. Preheat the air fryer to 400°F.
2. Use a vegetable peeler or mandoline to make long strips from the potato(es). You'll need anywhere from 8 to 12 strips per fillet, depending on the shape of the potato and of the salmon fillet.
3. Drape potato strips over a salmon fillet, overlapping the strips to create an even "crust." Tuck the potato strips under the fillet, overlapping the strips underneath to create as smooth a bottom as you can. Wrap the remaining fillet(s) in the same way.
4. Gently turn the fillets over. Generously coat the bottoms with olive oil spray. Turn them back seam side down and generously coat the tops with the oil spray. Sprinkle the salt and pepper over the wrapped fillets.
5. Use a nonstick-safe spatula to gently transfer the fillets seam side down to the basket. It helps to remove the basket from the machine and set it on your work surface (keeping in mind that the basket's hot). Leave as much air space as possible between the fillets. Air-fry undisturbed for 8 minutes, or until golden brown and crisp.
6. Use a nonstick-safe spatula to gently transfer the fillets to serving plates. Cool for a couple of minutes before serving.

Nutty Shrimp With Amaretto Glaze

Servings: 10
Cooking Time: 10 Minutes

Ingredients:

- 1 cup flour
- ½ teaspoon baking powder
- 1 teaspoon salt
- 2 eggs, beaten
- ½ cup milk
- 2 tablespoons olive or vegetable oil
- 2 cups sliced almonds
- 2 pounds large shrimp (about 32 to 40 shrimp), peeled and deveined, tails left on
- 2 cups amaretto liqueur

Directions:

1. Combine the flour, baking powder and salt in a large bowl. Add the eggs, milk and oil and stir until it forms a smooth batter. Coarsely crush the sliced almonds into a second shallow dish with your hands.
2. Dry the shrimp well with paper towels. Dip the shrimp into the batter and shake off any excess batter, leaving just enough to lightly coat the shrimp. Transfer the shrimp to the dish with the almonds and coat completely. Place the coated shrimp on a plate or baking sheet and when all the shrimp have been coated, freeze the shrimp for an 1 hour, or as long as a week before air-frying.
3. Preheat the air fryer to 400°F.
4. Transfer 8 frozen shrimp at a time to the air fryer basket. Air-fry for 6 minutes. Turn the shrimp over and air-fry for an additional 4 minutes. Repeat with the remaining shrimp.
5. While the shrimp are cooking, bring the Amaretto to a boil in a small saucepan on the stovetop. Lower the heat and simmer until it has reduced and thickened into a glaze – about 10 minutes.
6. Remove the shrimp from the air fryer and brush both sides with the warm amaretto glaze. Serve warm.

Coconut Jerk Shrimp

Servings:3
Cooking Time: 8 Minutes

Ingredients:
- 1 Large egg white(s)
- 1 teaspoon Purchased or homemade jerk dried seasoning blend (see the headnote)
- ¾ cup Plain panko bread crumbs (gluten-free, if a concern)
- ¾ cup Unsweetened shredded coconut
- 12 Large shrimp (20–25 per pound), peeled and deveined
- Coconut oil spray

Directions:
1. Preheat the air fryer to 375°F .
2. Whisk the egg white(s) and seasoning blend in a bowl until foamy. Add the shrimp and toss well to coat evenly.
3. Mix the bread crumbs and coconut on a dinner plate until well combined. Use kitchen tongs to pick up a shrimp, letting the excess egg white mixture slip back into the rest. Set the shrimp in the bread-crumb mixture. Turn several times to coat evenly and thoroughly. Set on a cutting board and continue coating the remainder of the shrimp.
4. Lightly coat all the shrimp on both sides with the coconut oil spray. Set them in the basket in one layer with as much space between them as possible. (You can even stand some up along the basket's wall in some models.) Air-fry undisturbed for 6 minutes, or until the coating is lightly browned. If the air fryer is at 360°F, you may need to add 2 minutes to the cooking time.
5. Use clean kitchen tongs to transfer the shrimp to a wire rack. Cool for only a minute or two before serving.

Fish-in-chips

Servings:4
Cooking Time: 11 Minutes

Ingredients:
- 1 cup All-purpose flour or potato starch
- 2 Large egg(s), well beaten
- 1½ cups (6 ounces) Crushed plain potato chips, preferably thick-cut or ruffled (gluten-free, if a concern)
- 4 4-ounce skinless cod fillets

Directions:
1. Preheat the air fryer to 400°F.
2. Set up and fill three shallow soup plates or small pie plates on your counter: one for the flour, one for the beaten egg(s), and one for the crushed potato chips.
3. Dip a piece of cod in the flour, turning it to coat on all sides, even the ends and sides. Gently shake off any excess flour, then dip it in the beaten egg(s). Gently turn to coat it on all sides, then let any excess egg slip back into the rest. Set the fillet in the crushed potato chips and turn several times and onto all sides, pressing gently to coat the fish. Dip it back in the egg(s), coating all sides but taking care that the coating doesn't slip off; then dip it back in the potato chips for a thick, even coating. Set it aside and coat more fillets in the same way.
4. When the machine is at temperature, set the fillets in the basket with as much air space between them as possible. Air-fry undisturbed for 11 minutes, until golden brown and firm but not hard.
5. Use kitchen tongs to transfer the fillets to a wire rack. Cool for just a minute or two before serving.

SANDWICHES AND BURGERS RECIPES

Sausage And Pepper Heros

Servings: 3
Cooking Time: 11 Minutes

Ingredients:
- 3 links (about 9 ounces total) Sweet Italian sausages (gluten-free, if a concern)
- 1½ Medium red or green bell pepper(s), stemmed, cored, and cut into ½-inch-wide strips
- 1 medium Yellow or white onion(s), peeled, halved, and sliced into thin half-moons
- 3 Long soft rolls, such as hero, hoagie, or Italian sub rolls (gluten-free, if a concern), split open lengthwise
- For garnishing Balsamic vinegar
- For garnishing Fresh basil leaves

Directions:
1. Preheat the air fryer to 400°F.
2. When the machine is at temperature, set the sausage links in the basket in one layer and air-fry undisturbed for 5 minutes.
3. Add the pepper strips and onions. Continue air-frying, tossing and rearranging everything about once every minute, for 5 minutes, or until the sausages are browned and an instant-read meat thermometer inserted into one of the links registers 160°F.
4. Use a nonstick-safe spatula and kitchen tongs to transfer the sausages and vegetables to a cutting board. Set the rolls cut side down in the basket in one layer (working in batches as necessary) and air-fry undisturbed for 1 minute, to toast the rolls a bit and warm them up. Set 1 sausage with some pepper strips and onions in each warm roll, sprinkle balsamic vinegar over the sandwich fillings, and garnish with basil leaves.

Chicken Gyros

Servings: 4

Cooking Time: 14 Minutes

Ingredients:

- 4 4- to 5-ounce boneless skinless chicken thighs, trimmed of any fat blobs
- 2 tablespoons Lemon juice
- 2 tablespoons Red wine vinegar
- 2 tablespoons Olive oil
- 2 teaspoons Dried oregano
- 2 teaspoons Minced garlic
- 1 teaspoon Table salt
- 1 teaspoon Ground black pepper
- 4 Pita pockets (gluten-free, if a concern)
- ½ cup Chopped tomatoes
- ½ cup Bottled regular, low-fat, or fat-free ranch dressing (gluten-free, if a concern)

Directions:

1. Mix the thighs, lemon juice, vinegar, oil, oregano, garlic, salt, and pepper in a zip-closed bag. Seal, gently massage the marinade into the meat through the plastic, and refrigerate for at least 2 hours or up to 6 hours. (Longer than that and the meat can turn rubbery.)
2. Set the plastic bag out on the counter (to make the contents a little less frigid). Preheat the air fryer to 375°F .
3. When the machine is at temperature, use kitchen tongs to place the thighs in the basket in one layer. Discard the marinade. Air-fry the chicken thighs undisturbed for 12 minutes, or until browned and an instant-read meat thermometer inserted into the thickest part of one thigh registers 165°F. You may need to air-fry the chicken 2 minutes longer if the machine's temperature is 360°F.
4. Use kitchen tongs to transfer the thighs to a cutting board. Cool for 5 minutes, then set one thigh in each of the pita pockets. Top each with 2 tablespoons chopped tomatoes and 2 tablespoons dressing. Serve warm.

Chicken Club Sandwiches

Servings: 3

Cooking Time: 15 Minutes

Ingredients:

- 3 5- to 6-ounce boneless skinless chicken breasts
- 6 Thick-cut bacon strips (gluten-free, if a concern)
- 3 Long soft rolls, such as hero, hoagie, or Italian sub rolls (gluten-free, if a concern)
- 3 tablespoons Regular, low-fat, or fat-free mayonnaise (gluten-free, if a concern)
- 3 Lettuce leaves, preferably romaine or iceberg
- 6 ¼-inch-thick tomato slices

Directions:

1. Preheat the air fryer to 375°F .
2. Wrap each chicken breast with 2 strips of bacon, spiraling the bacon around the meat, slightly overlapping the strips on each revolution. Start the second strip of bacon farther down the breast but on a line with the start of the first strip so they both end at a lined-up point on the chicken breast.
3. When the machine is at temperature, set the wrapped breasts bacon-seam side down in the basket with space between them. Air-fry undisturbed for 12 minutes, until the bacon is browned, crisp, and cooked through and an instant-read meat thermometer inserted into the center of a breast registers 165°F. You may need to add 2 minutes in the air fryer if the temperature is at 360°F.
4. Use kitchen tongs to transfer the breasts to a wire rack. Split the rolls open lengthwise and set them cut side down in the basket. Air-fry for 1 minute, or until warmed through.
5. Use kitchen tongs to transfer the rolls to a cutting board. Spread 1 tablespoon mayonnaise on the cut side of one half of each roll. Top with a chicken breast, lettuce leaf, and tomato slice. Serve warm.

Chicken Spiedies

Servings: 3

Cooking Time: 12 Minutes

Ingredients:

- 1¼ pounds Boneless skinless chicken thighs, trimmed of any fat blobs and cut into 2-inch pieces
- 3 tablespoons Red wine vinegar
- 2 tablespoons Olive oil
- 2 tablespoons Minced fresh mint leaves
- 2 tablespoons Minced fresh parsley leaves
- 2 teaspoons Minced fresh dill fronds
- ¾ teaspoon Fennel seeds
- ¾ teaspoon Table salt
- Up to a ¼ teaspoon Red pepper flakes
- 3 Long soft rolls, such as hero, hoagie, or Italian sub rolls (gluten-free, if a concern), split open lengthwise
- 4½ tablespoons Regular or low-fat mayonnaise (not fat-free; gluten-free, if a concern)
- 1½ tablespoons Distilled white vinegar
- 1½ teaspoons Ground black pepper

Directions:

1. Mix the chicken, vinegar, oil, mint, parsley, dill, fennel seeds, salt, and red pepper flakes in a zip-closed plastic bag. Seal, gently massage the marinade ingredients into the meat, and refrigerate for at least 2 hours or up to 6 hours. (Longer than that and the meat can turn rubbery.)
2. Set the plastic bag out on the counter (to make the contents a little less frigid). Preheat the air fryer to 400°F.
3. When the machine is at temperature, use kitchen tongs to set the chicken thighs in the basket (discard any remaining marinade) and air-fry undisturbed for 6 minutes. Turn the thighs over and continue air-frying undisturbed for 6 minutes more, until well browned, cooked through, and even a little crunchy.
4. Dump the contents of the basket onto a wire rack and cool for 2 or 3 minutes. Divide the chicken evenly between the rolls. Whisk the mayonnaise, vinegar, and black pepper in a small bowl until smooth. Drizzle this sauce over the chicken pieces in the rolls.

Asian Glazed Meatballs

Servings: 4

Cooking Time: 10 Minutes

Ingredients:

- 1 large shallot, finely chopped
- 2 cloves garlic, minced
- 1 tablespoon grated fresh ginger
- 2 teaspoons fresh thyme, finely chopped
- 1½ cups brown mushrooms, very finely chopped (a food processor works well here)
- 2 tablespoons soy sauce
- freshly ground black pepper
- 1 pound ground beef
- ½ pound ground pork
- 3 egg yolks
- 1 cup Thai sweet chili sauce (spring roll sauce)
- ¼ cup toasted sesame seeds
- 2 scallions, sliced

Directions:

1. Combine the shallot, garlic, ginger, thyme, mushrooms, soy sauce, freshly ground black pepper, ground beef and pork, and egg yolks in a bowl and mix the ingredients together. Gently shape the mixture into 24 balls, about the size of a golf ball.
2. Preheat the air fryer to 380°F.
3. Working in batches, air-fry the meatballs for 8 minutes, turning the meatballs over halfway through the cooking time. Drizzle some of the Thai sweet chili sauce on top of each meatball and return the basket to the air fryer, air-frying for another 2 minutes. Reserve the remaining Thai sweet chili sauce for serving.
4. As soon as the meatballs are done, sprinkle with toasted sesame seeds and transfer them to a serving platter. Scatter the scallions around and serve warm.

Reuben Sandwiches

Servings: 2
Cooking Time: 11 Minutes

Ingredients:

- ½ pound Sliced deli corned beef
- 4 teaspoons Regular or low-fat mayonnaise (not fat-free)
- 4 Rye bread slices
- 2 tablespoons plus 2 teaspoons Russian dressing
- ½ cup Purchased sauerkraut, squeezed by the handful over the sink to get rid of excess moisture
- 2 ounces (2 to 4 slices) Swiss cheese slices (optional)

Directions:

1. Set the corned beef in the basket, slip the basket into the machine, and heat the air fryer to 400°F. Air-fry undisturbed for 3 minutes from the time the basket is put in the machine, just to warm up the meat.
2. Use kitchen tongs to transfer the corned beef to a cutting board. Spread 1 teaspoon mayonnaise on one side of each slice of rye bread, rubbing the mayonnaise into the bread with a small flatware knife.
3. Place the bread slices mayonnaise side down on a cutting board. Spread the Russian dressing over the "dry" side of each slice. For one sandwich, top one slice of bread with the corned beef, sauerkraut, and cheese (if using). For two sandwiches, top two slices of bread each with half of the corned beef, sauerkraut, and cheese (if using). Close the sandwiches with the remaining bread, setting it mayonnaise side up on top.
4. Set the sandwich(es) in the basket and air-fry undisturbed for 8 minutes, or until browned and crunchy.
5. Use a nonstick-safe spatula, and perhaps a flatware fork for balance, to transfer the sandwich(es) to a cutting board. Cool for 2 or 3 minutes before slicing in half and serving.

White Bean Veggie Burgers

Servings: 3

Cooking Time: 13 Minutes

Ingredients:

- 1⅓ cups Drained and rinsed canned white beans
- 3 tablespoons Rolled oats (not quick-cooking or steel-cut; gluten-free, if a concern)
- 3 tablespoons Chopped walnuts
- 2 teaspoons Olive oil
- 2 teaspoons Lemon juice
- 1½ teaspoons Dijon mustard (gluten-free, if a concern)
- ¾ teaspoon Dried sage leaves
- ¼ teaspoon Table salt
- Olive oil spray
- 3 Whole-wheat buns or gluten-free whole-grain buns (if a concern), split open

Directions:

1. Preheat the air fryer to 400°F.
2. Place the beans, oats, walnuts, oil, lemon juice, mustard, sage, and salt in a food processor. Cover and process to make a coarse paste that will hold its shape, about like wet sugar-cookie dough, stopping the machine to scrape down the inside of the canister at least once.
3. Scrape down and remove the blade. With clean and wet hands, form the bean paste into two 4-inch patties for the small batch, three 4-inch patties for the medium, or four 4-inch patties for the large batch. Generously coat the patties on both sides with olive oil spray.
4. Set them in the basket with some space between them and air-fry undisturbed for 12 minutes, or until lightly brown and crisp at the edges. The tops of the burgers will feel firm to the touch.
5. Use a nonstick-safe spatula, and perhaps a flatware fork for balance, to transfer the burgers to a cutting board. Set the buns cut side down in the basket in one layer (working in batches as necessary) and air-fry undisturbed for 1 minute, to toast a bit and warm up. Serve the burgers warm in the buns.

Chicken Saltimbocca Sandwiches

Servings: 3
Cooking Time: 11 Minutes

Ingredients:

- 3 5- to 6-ounce boneless skinless chicken breasts
- 6 Thin prosciutto slices
- 6 Provolone cheese slices
- 3 Long soft rolls, such as hero, hoagie, or Italian sub rolls (gluten-free, if a concern), split open lengthwise
- 3 tablespoons Pesto, purchased or homemade (see the headnote)

Directions:

1. Preheat the air fryer to 400°F.
2. Wrap each chicken breast with 2 prosciutto slices, spiraling the prosciutto around the breast and overlapping the slices a bit to cover the breast. The prosciutto will stick to the chicken more readily than bacon does.
3. When the machine is at temperature, set the wrapped chicken breasts in the basket and air-fry undisturbed for 10 minutes, or until the prosciutto is frizzled and the chicken is cooked through.
4. Overlap 2 cheese slices on each breast. Air-fry undisturbed for 1 minute, or until melted. Take the basket out of the machine.
5. Smear the insides of the rolls with the pesto, then use kitchen tongs to put a wrapped and cheesy chicken breast in each roll.

Salmon Burgers

Servings: 3
Cooking Time: 8 Minutes

Ingredients:

- 1 pound 2 ounces Skinless salmon fillet, preferably fattier Atlantic salmon
- 1½ tablespoons Minced chives or the green part of a scallion
- ½ cup Plain panko bread crumbs (gluten-free, if a concern)
- 1½ teaspoons Dijon mustard (gluten-free, if a concern)
- 1½ teaspoons Drained and rinsed capers, minced
- 1½ teaspoons Lemon juice
- ¼ teaspoon Table salt
- ¼ teaspoon Ground black pepper
- Vegetable oil spray

Directions:

1. Preheat the air fryer to 375°F .
2. Cut the salmon into pieces that will fit in a food processor. Cover and pulse until coarsely chopped. Add the chives and pulse to combine, until the fish is ground but not a paste. Scrape down and remove the blade. Scrape the salmon mixture into a bowl. Add the bread crumbs, mustard, capers, lemon juice, salt, and pepper. Stir gently until well combined.
3. Use clean and dry hands to form the mixture into two 5-inch patties for a small batch, three 5-inch patties for a medium batch, or four 5-inch patties for a large one.
4. Coat both sides of each patty with vegetable oil spray. Set them in the basket in one layer and air-fry undisturbed for 8 minutes, or until browned and an instant-read meat thermometer inserted into the center of a burger registers 145°F.
5. Use a nonstick-safe spatula, and perhaps a flatware fork for balance, to transfer the burgers to a wire rack. Cool for 2 or 3 minutes before serving.

Turkey Burgers

Servings: 3
Cooking Time: 23 Minutes

Ingredients:

- 1 pound 2 ounces Ground turkey
- 6 tablespoons Frozen chopped spinach, thawed and squeezed dry
- 3 tablespoons Plain panko bread crumbs (gluten-free, if a concern)
- 1 tablespoon Dijon mustard (gluten-free, if a concern)
- 1½ teaspoons Minced garlic
- ¾ teaspoon Table salt
- ¾ teaspoon Ground black pepper
- Olive oil spray
- 3 Kaiser rolls (gluten-free, if a concern), split open

Directions:

1. Preheat the air fryer to 375°F .
2. Gently mix the ground turkey, spinach, bread crumbs, mustard, garlic, salt, and pepper in a large bowl until well combined, trying to keep some of the fibers of the ground turkey intact. Form into two 5-inch-wide patties for the small batch, three 5-inch patties for the medium batch, or four 5-inch patties for the large. Coat each side of the patties with olive oil spray.
3. Set the patties in in the basket in one layer and air-fry undisturbed for 20 minutes, or until an instant-read meat thermometer inserted into the center of a burger registers 165°F. You may need to add 2 minutes to the cooking time if the air fryer is at 360°F.
4. Use a nonstick-safe spatula, and perhaps a flatware fork for balance, to transfer the burgers to a cutting board. Set the buns cut side down in the basket in one layer (working in batches as necessary) and air-fry for 1 minute, to toast a bit and warm up. Serve the burgers warm in the buns.

Thai-style Pork Sliders

Servings: 4

Cooking Time: 15 Minutes

Ingredients:

- 11 ounces Ground pork
- 2½ tablespoons Very thinly sliced scallions, white and green parts
- 4 teaspoons Minced peeled fresh ginger
- 2½ teaspoons Fish sauce (gluten-free, if a concern)
- 2 teaspoons Thai curry paste (see the headnote; gluten-free, if a concern)
- 2 teaspoons Light brown sugar
- ¾ teaspoon Ground black pepper
- 4 Slider buns (gluten-free, if a concern)

Directions:

1. Preheat the air fryer to 375°F .
2. Gently mix the pork, scallions, ginger, fish sauce, curry paste, brown sugar, and black pepper in a bowl until well combined. With clean, wet hands, form about ⅓ cup of the pork mixture into a slider about 2½ inches in diameter. Repeat until you use up all the meat—3 sliders for the small batch, 4 for the medium, and 6 for the large. (Keep wetting your hands to help the patties adhere.)
3. When the machine is at temperature, set the sliders in the basket in one layer. Air-fry undisturbed for 14 minutes, or until the sliders are golden brown and caramelized at their edges and an instant-read meat thermometer inserted into the center of a slider registers 160°F.
4. Use a nonstick-safe spatula, and perhaps a flatware fork for balance, to transfer the sliders to a cutting board. Set the buns cut side down in the basket in one layer (working in batches as necessary) and air-fry undisturbed for 1 minute, to toast a bit and warm up. Serve the sliders warm in the buns.

VEGETARIANS RECIPES

Charred Cauliflower Tacos

Servings: 4
Cooking Time: 10 Minutes

Ingredients:
- 1 head cauliflower, washed and cut into florets
- 2 tablespoons avocado oil
- 2 teaspoons taco seasoning
- 1 medium avocado
- ½ teaspoon garlic powder
- ¼ teaspoon black pepper
- ¼ teaspoon salt
- 2 tablespoons chopped red onion
- 2 teaspoons fresh squeezed lime juice
- ¼ cup chopped cilantro
- Eight 6-inch corn tortillas
- ½ cup cooked corn
- ½ cup shredded purple cabbage

Directions:
1. Preheat the air fryer to 390°F.
2. In a large bowl, toss the cauliflower with the avocado oil and taco seasoning. Set the metal trivet inside the air fryer basket and liberally spray with olive oil.
3. Place the cauliflower onto the trivet and cook for 10 minutes, shaking every 3 minutes to allow for an even char.
4. While the cauliflower is cooking, prepare the avocado sauce. In a medium bowl, mash the avocado; then mix in the garlic powder, pepper, salt, and onion. Stir in the lime juice and cilantro; set aside.
5. Remove the cauliflower from the air fryer basket.
6. Place 1 tablespoon of avocado sauce in the middle of a tortilla, and top with corn, cabbage, and charred cauliflower. Repeat with the remaining tortillas. Serve immediately.

Egg Rolls

Servings: 4
Cooking Time: 8 Minutes

Ingredients:
- 1 clove garlic, minced
- 1 teaspoon sesame oil
- 1 teaspoon olive oil
- ½ cup chopped celery
- ½ cup grated carrots
- 2 green onions, chopped
- 2 ounces mushrooms, chopped
- 2 cups shredded Napa cabbage
- 1 teaspoon low-sodium soy sauce
- 1 teaspoon cornstarch
- salt
- 1 egg
- 1 tablespoon water
- 4 egg roll wraps
- olive oil for misting or cooking spray

Directions:
1. In a large skillet, sauté garlic in sesame and olive oils over medium heat for 1 minute.
2. Add celery, carrots, onions, and mushrooms to skillet. Cook 1 minute, stirring.
3. Stir in cabbage, cover, and cook for 1 minute or just until cabbage slightly wilts.
4. In a small bowl, mix soy sauce and cornstarch. Stir into vegetables to thicken. Remove from heat. Salt to taste if needed.
5. Beat together egg and water in a small bowl.
6. Divide filling into 4 portions and roll up in egg roll wraps. Brush all over with egg wash to seal.
7. Mist egg rolls very lightly with olive oil or cooking spray and place in air fryer basket.
8. Cook at 390°F for 4minutes. Turn over and cook 4 more minutes, until golden brown and crispy.

Quinoa Burgers With Feta Cheese And Dill

Servings: 6

Cooking Time: 10 Minutes

Ingredients:

- 1 cup quinoa (red, white or multi-colored)
- 1½ cups water
- 1 teaspoon salt
- freshly ground black pepper
- 1½ cups rolled oats
- 3 eggs, lightly beaten
- ¼ cup minced white onion
- ½ cup crumbled feta cheese
- ¼ cup chopped fresh dill
- salt and freshly ground black pepper
- vegetable or canola oil, in a spray bottle
- whole-wheat hamburger buns (or gluten-free hamburger buns*)
- arugula
- tomato, sliced
- red onion, sliced
- mayonnaise

Directions:

1. Make the quinoa: Rinse the quinoa in cold water in a saucepan, swirling it with your hand until any dry husks rise to the surface. Drain the quinoa as well as you can and then put the saucepan on the stovetop to dry and toast the quinoa. Turn the heat to medium-high and shake the pan regularly until you see the quinoa moving easily and can hear the seeds moving in the pan, indicating that they are dry. Add the water, salt and pepper. Bring the liquid to a boil and then reduce the heat to low or medium-low. You should see just a few bubbles, not a boil. Cover with a lid, leaving it askew and simmer for 20 minutes. Turn the heat off and fluff the quinoa with a fork. If there's any liquid left in the bottom of the pot, place it back on the burner for another 3 minutes or so. Spread the cooked quinoa out on a sheet pan to cool.

2. Combine the room temperature quinoa in a large bowl with the oats, eggs, onion, cheese and dill. Season with salt and pepper and mix well (remember that feta cheese is salty). Shape the mixture into 6 patties with flat sides (so they fit more easily into the air fryer). Add a little water or a few more rolled oats if necessary to get the mixture to be the right consistency to make patties.

3. Preheat the air-fryer to 400°F.

4. Spray both sides of the patties generously with oil and transfer them to the air fryer basket in one layer (you will probably have to cook these burgers in batches, depending on the size of your air fryer). Air-fry each batch at 400°F for 10 minutes, flipping the burgers over halfway through the cooking time.

5. Build your burger on the whole-wheat hamburger buns with arugula, tomato, red onion and mayonnaise.

Cheese Ravioli

Servings: 4
Cooking Time: 9 Minutes

Ingredients:
- 1 egg
- ¼ cup milk
- 1 cup breadcrumbs
- 2 teaspoons Italian seasoning
- ⅛ teaspoon ground rosemary
- ¼ teaspoon basil
- ¼ teaspoon parsley
- 9-ounce package uncooked cheese ravioli
- ¼ cup flour
- oil for misting or cooking spray

Directions:
1. Preheat air fryer to 390°F.
2. In a medium bowl, beat together egg and milk.
3. In a large plastic bag, mix together the breadcrumbs, Italian seasoning, rosemary, basil, and parsley.
4. Place all the ravioli and the flour in a bag or a bowl with a lid and shake to coat.
5. Working with a handful at a time, drop floured ravioli into egg wash. Remove ravioli, letting excess drip off, and place in bag with breadcrumbs.
6. When all ravioli are in the breadcrumbs' bag, shake well to coat all pieces.
7. Dump enough ravioli into air fryer basket to form one layer. Mist with oil or cooking spray. Dump the remaining ravioli on top of the first layer and mist with oil.
8. Cook for 5minutes. Shake well and spray with oil. Break apart any ravioli stuck together and spray any spots you missed the first time.
9. Cook 4 minutes longer, until ravioli puff up and are crispy golden brown.

Falafel

Servings: 4

Cooking Time: 10 Minutes

Ingredients:

- 1 cup dried chickpeas
- ½ onion, chopped
- 1 clove garlic
- ¼ cup fresh parsley leaves
- 1 teaspoon salt
- ¼ teaspoon crushed red pepper flakes
- 1 teaspoon ground cumin
- ½ teaspoon ground coriander
- 1 to 2 tablespoons flour
- olive oil
- Tomato Salad
- 2 tomatoes, seeds removed and diced
- ½ cucumber, finely diced
- ¼ red onion, finely diced and rinsed with water
- 1 teaspoon red wine vinegar
- 1 tablespoon olive oil
- salt and freshly ground black pepper
- 2 tablespoons chopped fresh parsley

Directions:

1. Cover the chickpeas with water and let them soak overnight on the counter. Then drain the chickpeas and put them in a food processor, along with the onion, garlic, parsley, spices and 1 tablespoon of flour. Pulse in the food processor until the mixture has broken down into a coarse paste consistency. The mixture should hold together when you pinch it. Add more flour as needed, until you get this consistency.
2. Scoop portions of the mixture (about 2 tablespoons in size) and shape into balls. Place the balls on a plate and refrigerate for at least 30 minutes. You should have between 12 and 14 balls.
3. Preheat the air fryer to 380°F.
4. Spray the falafel balls with oil and place them in the air fryer. Air-fry for 10 minutes, rolling them over and spraying them with oil again halfway through the cooking time so that they cook and brown evenly.
5. Serve with pita bread, hummus, cucumbers, hot peppers, tomatoes or any other fillings you might like.

Veggie Fried Rice

Servings: 4
Cooking Time: 25 Minutes

Ingredients:
- 1 cup cooked brown rice
- ⅓ cup chopped onion
- ½ cup chopped carrots
- ½ cup chopped bell peppers
- ½ cup chopped broccoli florets
- 3 tablespoons low-sodium soy sauce
- 1 tablespoon sesame oil
- 1 teaspoon ground ginger
- 1 teaspoon ground garlic powder
- ½ teaspoon black pepper
- ⅛ teaspoon salt
- 2 large eggs

Directions:
1. Preheat the air fryer to 370°F.
2. In a large bowl, mix together the brown rice, onions, carrots, bell pepper, and broccoli.
3. In a small bowl, whisk together the soy sauce, sesame oil, ginger, garlic powder, pepper, salt, and eggs.
4. Pour the egg mixture into the rice and vegetable mixture and mix together.
5. Liberally spray a 7-inch springform pan (or compatible air fryer dish) with olive oil. Add the rice mixture to the pan and cover with aluminum foil.
6. Place a metal trivet into the air fryer basket and set the pan on top. Cook for 15 minutes. Carefully remove the pan from basket, discard the foil, and mix the rice. Return the rice to the air fryer basket, turning down the temperature to 350°F and cooking another 10 minutes.
7. Remove and let cool 5 minutes. Serve warm.

Broccoli Cheddar Stuffed Potatoes

Servings: 2

Cooking Time: 42 Minutes

Ingredients:

- 2 large russet potatoes, scrubbed
- 1 tablespoon olive oil
- salt and freshly ground black pepper
- 2 tablespoons butter
- ¼ cup sour cream
- 3 tablespoons half-and-half (or milk)
- 1¼ cups grated Cheddar cheese, divided
- ¾ teaspoon salt
- freshly ground black pepper
- 1 cup frozen baby broccoli florets, thawed and drained

Directions:

1. Preheat the air fryer to 400°F.
2. Rub the potatoes all over with olive oil and season generously with salt and freshly ground black pepper. Transfer the potatoes into the air fryer basket and air-fry for 30 minutes, turning the potatoes over halfway through the cooking process.
3. Remove the potatoes from the air fryer and let them rest for 5 minutes. Cut a large oval out of the top of both potatoes. Leaving half an inch of potato flesh around the edge of the potato, scoop the inside of the potato out and into a large bowl to prepare the potato filling. Mash the scooped potato filling with a fork and add the butter, sour cream, half-and-half, 1 cup of the grated Cheddar cheese, salt and pepper to taste. Mix well and then fold in the broccoli florets.
4. Stuff the hollowed out potato shells with the potato and broccoli mixture. Mound the filling high in the potatoes – you will have more filling than room in the potato shells.
5. Transfer the stuffed potatoes back to the air fryer basket and air-fry at 360°F for 10 minutes. Sprinkle the remaining Cheddar cheese on top of each stuffed potato, lower the heat to 330°F and air-fry for an additional minute or two to melt cheese.

Parmesan Portobello Mushroom Caps

Servings: 2

Cooking Time: 14 Minutes

Ingredients:
- ¼ cup flour*
- 1 egg, lightly beaten
- 1 cup seasoned breadcrumbs*
- 2 large portobello mushroom caps, stems and gills removed
- olive oil, in a spray bottle
- ½ cup tomato sauce
- ¾ cup grated mozzarella cheese
- 1 tablespoon grated Parmesan cheese
- 1 tablespoon chopped fresh basil or parsley

Directions:
1. Set up a dredging station with three shallow dishes. Place the flour in the first shallow dish, egg in the second dish and breadcrumbs in the last dish. Dredge the mushrooms in flour, then dip them into the egg and finally press them into the breadcrumbs to coat on all sides. Spray both sides of the coated mushrooms with olive oil.
2. Preheat the air fryer to 400°F.
3. Air-fry the mushrooms at 400°F for 10 minutes, turning them over halfway through the cooking process.
4. Fill the underside of the mushrooms with the tomato sauce and then top the sauce with the mozzarella and Parmesan cheeses. Reset the air fryer temperature to 350°F and air-fry for an additional 4 minutes, until the cheese has melted and is slightly browned.
5. Serve the mushrooms with pasta tossed with tomato sauce and garnish with some chopped fresh basil or parsley.

Tacos

Servings: 24

Cooking Time: 8 Minutes Per Batch

Ingredients:

- 1 24-count package 4-inch corn tortillas
- 1½ cups refried beans (about ¾ of a 15-ounce can)
- 4 ounces sharp Cheddar cheese, grated
- ½ cup salsa
- oil for misting or cooking spray

Directions:

1. Preheat air fryer to 390°F.
2. Wrap refrigerated tortillas in damp paper towels and microwave for 30 to 60 seconds to warm. If necessary, rewarm tortillas as you go to keep them soft enough to fold without breaking.
3. Working with one tortilla at a time, top with 1 tablespoon of beans, 1 tablespoon of grated cheese, and 1 teaspoon of salsa. Fold over and press down very gently on the center. Press edges firmly all around to seal. Spray both sides with oil or cooking spray.
4. Cooking in two batches, place half the tacos in the air fryer basket. To cook 12 at a time, you may need to stand them upright and lean some against the sides of basket. It's okay if they're crowded as long as you leave a little room for air to circulate around them.
5. Cook for 8 minutes or until golden brown and crispy.
6. Repeat steps 4 and 5 to cook remaining tacos.

Vegetable Hand Pies

Servings: 8
Cooking Time: 10 Minutes Per Batch

Ingredients:

- ¾ cup vegetable broth
- 8 ounces potatoes
- ¾ cup frozen chopped broccoli, thawed
- ¼ cup chopped mushrooms
- 1 tablespoon cornstarch
- 1 tablespoon milk
- 1 can organic flaky biscuits (8 large biscuits)
- oil for misting or cooking spray

Directions:

1. Place broth in medium saucepan over low heat.
2. While broth is heating, grate raw potato into a bowl of water to prevent browning. You will need ¾ cup grated potato.
3. Roughly chop the broccoli.
4. Drain potatoes and put them in the broth along with the broccoli and mushrooms. Cook on low for 5 minutes.
5. Dissolve cornstarch in milk, then stir the mixture into the broth. Cook about a minute, until mixture thickens a little. Remove from heat and cool slightly.
6. Separate each biscuit into 2 rounds. Divide vegetable mixture evenly over half the biscuit rounds, mounding filling in the center of each.
7. Top the four rounds with filling, then the other four rounds and crimp the edges together with a fork.
8. Spray both sides with oil or cooking spray and place 4 pies in a single layer in the air fryer basket.
9. Cook at 330°F for approximately 10 minutes.
10. Repeat with the remaining biscuits. The second batch may cook more quickly because the fryer will be hot.

Mexican Twice Air-fried Sweet Potatoes

Servings: 2

Cooking Time: 42 Minutes

Ingredients:

- 2 large sweet potatoes
- olive oil
- salt and freshly ground black pepper
- ⅓ cup diced red onion
- ⅓ cup diced red bell pepper
- ½ cup canned black beans, drained and rinsed
- ½ cup corn kernels, fresh or frozen
- ½ teaspoon chili powder
- 1½ cups grated pepper jack cheese, divided
- Jalapeño peppers, sliced

Directions:

1. Preheat the air fryer to 400°F.
2. Rub the outside of the sweet potatoes with olive oil and season with salt and freshly ground black pepper. Transfer the potatoes into the air fryer basket and air-fry at 400°F for 30 minutes, rotating the potatoes a few times during the cooking process.
3. While the potatoes are air-frying, start the potato filling. Preheat a large sauté pan over medium heat on the stovetop. Add the onion and pepper and sauté for a few minutes, until the vegetables start to soften. Add the black beans, corn, and chili powder and sauté for another 3 minutes. Set the mixture aside.
4. Remove the sweet potatoes from the air fryer and let them rest for 5 minutes. Slice off one inch of the flattest side of both potatoes. Scrape the potato flesh out of the potatoes, leaving half an inch of potato flesh around the edge of the potato. Place all the potato flesh into a large bowl and mash it with a fork. Add the black bean mixture and 1 cup of the pepper jack cheese to the mashed sweet potatoes. Season with salt and freshly ground black pepper and mix well. Stuff the hollowed out potato shells with the black bean and sweet potato mixture, mounding the filling high in the potatoes.
5. Transfer the stuffed potatoes back into the air fryer basket and air-fry at 370°F for 10 minutes. Sprinkle the remaining cheese on top of each stuffed potato, lower the heat to 340°F and air-fry for an additional 2 minutes to melt the cheese. Top with a couple slices of Jalapeño pepper and serve warm with a green salad.

DESSERTS AND SWEETS

Chocolate Macaroons

Servings: 16
Cooking Time: 8 Minutes

Ingredients:
- 2 Large egg white(s), at room temperature
- ⅛ teaspoon Table salt
- ½ cup Granulated white sugar
- 1½ cups Unsweetened shredded coconut
- 3 tablespoons Unsweetened cocoa powder

Directions:
1. Preheat the air fryer to 375°F .
2. Using an electric mixer at high speed, beat the egg white(s) and salt in a medium or large bowl until stiff peaks can be formed when the turned-off beaters are dipped into the mixture.
3. Still working with the mixer at high speed, beat in the sugar in a slow stream until the meringue is shiny and thick.
4. Scrape down and remove the beaters. Fold in the coconut and cocoa with a rubber spatula until well combined, working carefully to deflate the meringue as little as possible.
5. Scoop up 2 tablespoons of the mixture. Wet your clean hands and roll that little bit of coconut bliss into a ball. Set it aside and continue making more balls: 7 more for a small batch, 15 more for a medium batch, or 23 more for a large one.
6. Line the bottom of the machine's basket or the basket attachment with parchment paper. Set the balls on the parchment with as much air space between them as possible. Air-fry undisturbed for 8 minutes, or until dry, set, and lightly browned.
7. Use a nonstick-safe spatula to transfer the macaroons to a wire rack. Cool for at least 10 minutes before serving. Or cool to room temperature, about 30 minutes, then store in a sealed container at room temperature for up to 3 days.

Fudgy Brownie Cake

Servings: 6

Cooking Time: 25-35 Minutes

Ingredients:

- 6½ tablespoons All-purpose flour
- ¼ cup plus 1 teaspoon Unsweetened cocoa powder
- ½ teaspoon Baking powder
- ¼ teaspoon Table salt
- 6½ tablespoons Butter, at room temperature
- 9½ tablespoons Granulated white sugar
- 1 egg plus 1 large egg white Large egg(s)
- ¾ teaspoon Vanilla extract
- Baking spray (see here)

Directions:

1. Preheat the air fryer to 325°F (or 330°F, if that's the closest setting).
2. Mix the flour, cocoa powder, baking powder, and salt in a small bowl until well combined.
3. Using an electric hand mixer at medium speed, beat the butter and sugar in a medium bowl until creamy and smooth, about 3 minutes, occasionally scraping down the inside of the bowl.
4. Beat in the egg(s) and the white or yolk (as necessary), as well as the vanilla, until smooth. Turn off the beaters and add the flour mixture. Beat at low speed until thick and smooth.
5. Use the baking spray to generously coat the inside of a 6-inch round cake pan for a small batch, a 7-inch round cake pan for a medium batch, or an 8-inch round cake pan for a large batch. Scrape and spread the batter into the pan, smoothing the batter out to an even layer.
6. Set the pan in the basket and air-fry for 25 minutes for a 6-inch layer, 30 minutes for a 7-inch layer, or 35 minutes for an 8-inch layer, or until the cake is set but soft to the touch. Start checking it at the 20-minute mark to know where you are.
7. Use hot pads or silicone baking mitts to transfer the cake pan to a wire rack. Cool for at least 1 hour or up to 4 hours. Using a nonstick-safe knife, slice the cake into wedges right in the pan and lift them out one by one.

Coconut Crusted Bananas With Pineapple Sauce

Servings: 4

Cooking Time: 5 Minutes

Ingredients:

- Pineapple Sauce
- 1½ cups puréed fresh pineapple
- 2 tablespoons sugar
- juice of 1 lemon
- ¼ teaspoon ground cinnamon
- 3 firm bananas
- ¼ cup sweetened condensed milk
- 1¼ cups shredded coconut
- ⅓ cup crushed graham crackers (crumbs)*
- vegetable or canola oil, in a spray bottle
- vanilla frozen yogurt or ice cream

Directions:

1. Make the pineapple sauce by combining the pineapple, sugar, lemon juice and cinnamon in a saucepan. Simmer the mixture on the stovetop for 20 minutes, and then set it aside.
2. Slice the bananas diagonally into ½-inch thick slices and place them in a bowl. Pour the sweetened condensed milk into the bowl and toss the bananas gently to coat. Combine the coconut and graham cracker crumbs together in a shallow dish. Remove the banana slices from the condensed milk and let any excess milk drip off. Dip the banana slices in the coconut and crumb mixture to coat both sides. Spray the coated slices with oil.
3. Preheat the air fryer to 400°F.
4. Grease the bottom of the air fryer basket with a little oil. Air-fry the bananas in batches at 400°F for 5 minutes, turning them over halfway through the cooking time. Air-fry until the bananas are golden brown on both sides.
5. Serve warm over vanilla frozen yogurt with some of the pineapple sauce spooned over top.

Mixed Berry Hand Pies

Servings: 4
Cooking Time: 15 Minutes

Ingredients:
- ¾ cup sugar
- ½ teaspoon ground cinnamon
- 1 tablespoon cornstarch
- 1 cup blueberries
- 1 cup blackberries
- 1 cup raspberries, divided
- 1 teaspoon water
- 1 package refrigerated pie dough (or your own homemade pie dough)
- 1 egg, beaten

Directions:
1. Combine the sugar, cinnamon, and cornstarch in a small saucepan. Add the blueberries, blackberries, and ½ cup of the raspberries. Toss the berries gently to coat them evenly. Add the teaspoon of water to the saucepan and turn the stovetop on to medium-high heat, stirring occasionally. Once the berries break down, release their juice and start to simmer (about 5 minutes), simmer for another couple of minutes and then transfer the mixture to a bowl, stir in the remaining ½ cup of raspberries and let it cool.
2. Preheat the air fryer to 370°F.
3. Cut the pie dough into four 5-inch circles and four 6-inch circles.
4. Spread the 6-inch circles on a flat surface. Divide the berry filling between all four circles. Brush the perimeter of the dough circles with a little water. Place the 5-inch circles on top of the filling and press the perimeter of the dough circles together to seal. Roll the edges of the bottom circle up over the top circle to make a crust around the filling. Press a fork around the crust to make decorative indentations and to seal the crust shut. Brush the pies with egg wash and sprinkle a little sugar on top. Poke a small hole in the center of each pie with a paring knife to vent the dough.
5. Air-fry two pies at a time. Brush or spray the air fryer basket with oil and place the pies into the basket. Air-fry for 9 minutes. Turn the pies over and air-fry for another 6 minutes. Serve warm or at room temperature.

Blueberry Crisp

Servings: 6
Cooking Time: 13 Minutes

Ingredients:

- 3 cups Fresh or thawed frozen blueberries
- ⅓ cup Granulated white sugar
- 1 tablespoon Instant tapioca
- ⅓ cup All-purpose flour
- ⅓ cup Rolled oats (not quick-cooking or steel-cut)
- ⅓ cup Chopped walnuts or pecans
- ⅓ cup Packed light brown sugar
- 5 tablespoons plus 1 teaspoon (⅔ stick) Butter, melted and cooled
- ¾ teaspoon Ground cinnamon
- ¼ teaspoon Table salt

Directions:

1. Preheat the air fryer to 400°F.
2. Mix the blueberries, granulated white sugar, and instant tapioca in a 6-inch round cake pan for a small batch, a 7-inch round cake pan for a medium batch, or an 8-inch round cake pan for a large batch.
3. When the machine is at temperature, set the cake pan in the basket and air-fry undisturbed for 5 minutes, or just until the blueberries begin to bubble.
4. Meanwhile, mix the flour, oats, nuts, brown sugar, butter, cinnamon, and salt in a medium bowl until well combined.
5. When the blueberries have begun to bubble, crumble this flour mixture evenly on top. Continue air-frying undisturbed for 8 minutes, or until the topping has browned a bit and the filling is bubbling.
6. Use two hot pads or silicone baking mitts to transfer the cake pan to a wire rack. Cool for at least 10 minutes or to room temperature before serving.

Fried Snickers Bars

Servings:8

Cooking Time: 4 Minutes

Ingredients:
- ⅓ cup All-purpose flour
- 1 Large egg white(s), beaten until foamy
- 1½ cups (6 ounces) Vanilla wafer cookie crumbs
- 8 Fun-size (0.6-ounce/17-gram) Snickers bars, frozen
- Vegetable oil spray

Directions:
1. Preheat the air fryer to 400°F.
2. Set up and fill three shallow soup plates or small pie plates on your counter: one for the flour, one for the beaten egg white(s), and one for the cookie crumbs.
3. Unwrap the frozen candy bars. Dip one in the flour, turning it to coat on all sides. Gently shake off any excess, then set it in the beaten egg white(s). Turn it to coat all sides, even the ends, then let any excess egg white slip back into the rest. Set the candy bar in the cookie crumbs. Turn to coat on all sides, even the ends. Dip the candy bar back in the egg white(s) a second time, then into the cookie crumbs a second time, making sure you have an even coating all around. Coat the covered candy bar all over with vegetable oil spray. Set aside so you can dip and coat the remaining candy bars.
4. Set the coated candy bars in the basket with as much air space between them as possible. Air-fry undisturbed for 4 minutes, or until golden brown.
5. Remove the basket from the machine and let the candy bars cool in the basket for 10 minutes. Use a nonstick-safe spatula to transfer them to a wire rack and cool for 5 minutes more before chowing down.

Easy Churros

Servings: 12
Cooking Time: 10 Minutes

Ingredients:

- ½ cup Water
- 4 tablespoons (¼ cup/½ stick) Butter
- ¼ teaspoon Table salt
- ½ cup All-purpose flour
- 2 Large egg(s)
- ¼ cup Granulated white sugar
- 2 teaspoons Ground cinnamon

Directions:

1. Bring the water, butter, and salt to a boil in a small saucepan set over high heat, stirring occasionally.
2. When the butter has fully melted, reduce the heat to medium and stir in the flour to form a dough. Continue cooking, stirring constantly, to dry out the dough until it coats the bottom and sides of the pan with a film, even a crust. Remove the pan from the heat, scrape the dough into a bowl, and cool for 15 minutes.
3. Using an electric hand mixer at medium speed, beat in the egg, or eggs one at a time, until the dough is smooth and firm enough to hold its shape.
4. Mix the sugar and cinnamon in a small bowl. Scoop up 1 tablespoon of the dough and roll it in the sugar mixture to form a small, coated tube about ½ inch in diameter and 2 inches long. Set it aside and make 5 more tubes for the small batch or 11 more for the large one.
5. Set the tubes on a plate and freeze for 20 minutes. Meanwhile, Preheat the air fryer to 375°F .
6. Set 3 frozen tubes in the basket for a small batch or 6 for a large one with as much air space between them as possible. Air-fry undisturbed for 10 minutes, or until puffed, brown, and set.
7. Use kitchen tongs to transfer the churros to a wire rack to cool for at least 5 minutes. Meanwhile, air-fry and cool the second batch of churros in the same way.

Giant Oatmeal–peanut Butter Cookie

Servings: 4

Cooking Time: 18 Minutes

Ingredients:

- 1 cup Rolled oats (not quick-cooking or steel-cut oats)
- ½ cup All-purpose flour
- ½ teaspoon Ground cinnamon
- ½ teaspoon Baking soda
- ⅓ cup Packed light brown sugar
- ¼ cup Solid vegetable shortening
- 2 tablespoons Natural-style creamy peanut butter
- 3 tablespoons Granulated white sugar
- 2 tablespoons (or 1 small egg, well beaten) Pasteurized egg substitute, such as Egg Beaters
- ⅓ cup Roasted, salted peanuts, chopped
- Baking spray

Directions:

1. Preheat the air fryer to 350°F .
2. Stir the oats, flour, cinnamon, and baking soda in a bowl until well combined.
3. Using an electric hand mixer at medium speed, beat the brown sugar, shortening, peanut butter, granulated white sugar, and egg substitute or egg (as applicable) until smooth and creamy, about 3 minutes, scraping down the inside of the bowl occasionally.
4. Scrape down and remove the beaters. Fold in the flour mixture and peanuts with a rubber spatula just until all the flour is moistened and the peanut bits are evenly distributed in the dough.
5. For a small air fryer, coat the inside of a 6-inch round cake pan with baking spray. For a medium air fryer, coat the inside of a 7-inch round cake pan with baking spray. And for a large air fryer, coat the inside of an 8-inch round cake pan with baking spray. Scrape and gently press the dough into the prepared pan, spreading it into an even layer to the perimeter.
6. Set the pan in the basket and air-fry undisturbed for 18 minutes, or until well browned.
7. Transfer the pan to a wire rack and cool for 15 minutes. Loosen the cookie from the perimeter with a spatula, then invert the pan onto a cutting board and let the cookie come free. Remove the pan and reinvert the cookie onto the wire rack. Cool for 5 minutes more before slicing into wedges to serve.

Coconut-custard Pie

Servings: 4
Cooking Time: 20 Minutes

Ingredients:

- 1 cup milk
- ¼ cup plus 2 tablespoons sugar
- ¼ cup biscuit baking mix
- 1 teaspoon vanilla
- 2 eggs
- 2 tablespoons melted butter
- cooking spray
- ½ cup shredded, sweetened coconut

Directions:

1. Place all ingredients except coconut in a medium bowl.
2. Using a hand mixer, beat on high speed for 3minutes.
3. Let sit for 5minutes.
4. Preheat air fryer to 330°F.
5. Spray a 6-inch round or 6 x 6-inch square baking pan with cooking spray and place pan in air fryer basket.
6. Pour filling into pan and sprinkle coconut over top.
7. Cook pie at 330°F for 20 minutes or until center sets.

Fried Cannoli Wontons

Servings: 10
Cooking Time: 8 Minutes

Ingredients:

- 8 ounces Neufchâtel cream cheese
- ¼ cup powdered sugar
- 1 teaspoon vanilla extract
- ¼ teaspoon salt
- ¼ cup mini chocolate chips
- 2 tablespoons chopped pecans (optional)
- 20 wonton wrappers
- ¼ cup filtered water

Directions:

1. Preheat the air fryer to 370°F.
2. In a large bowl, use a hand mixer to combine the cream cheese with the powdered sugar, vanilla, and salt. Fold in the chocolate chips and pecans. Set aside.
3. Lay the wonton wrappers out on a flat, smooth surface and place a bowl with the filtered water next to them.
4. Use a teaspoon to evenly divide the cream cheese mixture among the 20 wonton wrappers, placing the batter in the center of the wontons.
5. Wet the tip of your index finger, and gently moisten the outer edges of the wrapper. Then fold each wrapper until it creates a secure pocket.
6. Liberally spray the air fryer basket with olive oil mist.
7. Place the wontons into the basket, and cook for 5 to 8 minutes. When the outer edges begin to brown, remove the wontons from the air fryer basket. Repeat cooking with remaining wontons.
8. Serve warm.

Nutella® Torte

Servings: 6
Cooking Time: 55 Minutes

Ingredients:
- ¼ cup unsalted butter, softened
- ½ cup sugar
- 2 eggs
- 1 teaspoon vanilla
- 1¼ cups Nutella® (or other chocolate hazelnut spread), divided
- ¼ cup flour
- 1 teaspoon baking powder
- ¼ teaspoon salt
- dark chocolate fudge topping
- coarsely chopped toasted hazelnuts

Directions:
1. Cream the butter and sugar together with an electric hand mixer until light and fluffy. Add the eggs, vanilla, and ¾ cup of the Nutella® and mix until combined. Combine the flour, baking powder and salt together, and add these dry ingredients to the butter mixture, beating for 1 minute.
2. Preheat the air fryer to 350°F.
3. Grease a 7-inch cake pan with butter and then line the bottom of the pan with a circle of parchment paper. Grease the parchment paper circle as well. Pour the batter into the prepared cake pan and wrap the pan completely with aluminum foil. Lower the pan into the air fryer basket with an aluminum sling (fold a piece of aluminum foil into a strip about 2-inches wide by 24-inches long). Fold the ends of the aluminum foil over the top of the dish before returning the basket to the air fryer. Air-fry for 30 minutes. Remove the foil and air-fry for another 25 minutes.
4. Remove the cake from air fryer and let it cool for 10 minutes. Invert the cake onto a plate, remove the parchment paper and invert the cake back onto a serving platter. While the cake is still warm, spread the remaining ½ cup of Nutella® over the top of the cake. Melt the dark chocolate fudge in the microwave for about 10 seconds so it melts enough to be pourable. Drizzle the sauce on top of the cake in a zigzag motion. Turn the cake 90 degrees and drizzle more sauce in zigzags perpendicular to the first zigzags. Garnish the edges of the torte with the toasted hazelnuts and serve.

BREAD AND BREAKFAST

Spinach And Artichoke White Pizza

Servings: 2
Cooking Time: 18 Minutes

Ingredients:

- olive oil
- 3 cups fresh spinach
- 2 cloves garlic, minced, divided
- 1 (6- to 8-ounce) pizza dough ball*
- ½ cup grated mozzarella cheese
- ¼ cup grated Fontina cheese
- ¼ cup artichoke hearts, coarsely chopped
- 2 tablespoons grated Parmesan cheese
- ¼ teaspoon dried oregano
- salt and freshly ground black pepper

Directions:

1. Heat the oil in a medium sauté pan on the stovetop. Add the spinach and half the minced garlic to the pan and sauté for a few minutes, until the spinach has wilted. Remove the sautéed spinach from the pan and set it aside.
2. Preheat the air fryer to 390°F.
3. Cut out a piece of aluminum foil the same size as the bottom of the air fryer basket. Brush the foil circle with olive oil. Shape the dough into a circle and place it on top of the foil. Dock the dough by piercing it several times with a fork. Brush the dough lightly with olive oil and transfer it into the air fryer basket with the foil on the bottom.
4. Air-fry the plain pizza dough for 6 minutes. Turn the dough over, remove the aluminum foil and brush again with olive oil. Air-fry for an additional 4 minutes.
5. Sprinkle the mozzarella and Fontina cheeses over the dough. Top with the spinach and artichoke hearts. Sprinkle the Parmesan cheese and dried oregano on top and drizzle with olive oil. Lower the temperature of the air fryer to 350°F and cook for 8 minutes, until the cheese has melted and is lightly browned. Season to taste with salt and freshly ground black pepper.

Egg And Sausage Crescent Rolls

Servings: 8

Cooking Time: 11 Minutes

Ingredients:

- 5 large eggs
- ¼ teaspoon black pepper
- ¼ teaspoon salt
- 1 tablespoon milk
- ¼ cup shredded cheddar cheese
- One 8-ounce package refrigerated crescent rolls
- 4 tablespoon pesto sauce
- 8 fully cooked breakfast sausage links, defrosted

Directions:

1. Preheat the air fryer to 320°F.
2. In a medium bowl, crack the eggs and whisk with the pepper, salt, and milk. Pour into a frying pan over medium heat and scramble. Just before the eggs are done, turn off the heat and add in the cheese. Continue to cook until the cheese has melted and the eggs are finished (about 5 minutes total). Remove from the heat.
3. Remove the crescent rolls from the package and press them flat onto a clean surface lightly dusted with flour. Add 1½ teaspoons of pesto sauce across the center of each roll. Place equal portions of eggs across all 8 rolls. Then top each roll with a sausage link and roll the dough up tight so it resembles the crescent-roll shape.
4. Lightly spray your air fryer basket with olive oil mist and place the rolls on top. Bake for 6 minutes or until the tops of the rolls are lightly browned.
5. Remove and let cool 3 to 5 minutes before serving.

Blueberry Muffins

Servings: 8
Cooking Time: 14 Minutes

Ingredients:

- 1⅓ cups flour
- ½ cup sugar
- 2 teaspoons baking powder
- ¼ teaspoon salt
- ⅓ cup canola oil
- 1 egg
- ½ cup milk
- ⅔ cup blueberries, fresh or frozen and thawed
- 8 foil muffin cups including paper liners

Directions:

1. Preheat air fryer to 330°F.
2. In a medium bowl, stir together flour, sugar, baking powder, and salt.
3. In a separate bowl, combine oil, egg, and milk and mix well.
4. Add egg mixture to dry ingredients and stir just until moistened.
5. Gently stir in blueberries.
6. Spoon batter evenly into muffin cups.
7. Place 4 muffin cups in air fryer basket and bake at 330°F for 14 minutes or until tops spring back when touched lightly.
8. Repeat previous step to cook remaining muffins.

Bacon Puff Pastry Pinwheels

Servings: 8
Cooking Time: 10 Minutes

Ingredients:
- 1 sheet of puff pastry
- 2 tablespoons maple syrup
- ¼ cup brown sugar
- 8 slices bacon (not thick cut)
- coarsely cracked black pepper
- vegetable oil

Directions:
1. On a lightly floured surface, roll the puff pastry out into a square that measures roughly 10 inches wide by however long your bacon strips are (usually about 11 inches). Cut the pastry into eight even strips.
2. Brush the strips of pastry with the maple syrup and sprinkle the brown sugar on top, leaving 1 inch of dough exposed at the far end of each strip. Place a slice of bacon on each strip of puff pastry, letting 1/8-inch of the length of bacon hang over the edge of the pastry. Season generously with coarsely ground black pepper.
3. With the exposed end of the pastry strips away from you, roll the bacon and pastry strips up into pinwheels. Dab a little water on the exposed end of the pastry and pinch it to the pinwheel to seal the pastry shut.
4. Preheat the air fryer to 360°F.
5. Brush or spray the air fryer basket with a little vegetable oil. Place the pinwheels into the basket and air-fry at 360°F for 8 minutes. Turn the pinwheels over and air-fry for another 2 minutes to brown the bottom. Serve warm.

Ham And Cheddar Gritters

Servings: 6
Cooking Time: 12 Minutes

Ingredients:

- 4 cups water
- 1 cup quick-cooking grits
- ¼ teaspoon salt
- 2 tablespoons butter
- 2 cups grated Cheddar cheese, divided
- 1 cup finely diced ham
- 1 tablespoon chopped chives
- salt and freshly ground black pepper
- 1 egg, beaten
- 2 cups panko breadcrumbs
- vegetable oil

Directions:

1. Bring the water to a boil in a saucepan. Whisk in the grits and ¼ teaspoon of salt, and cook for 7 minutes until the grits are soft. Remove the pan from the heat and stir in the butter and 1 cup of the grated Cheddar cheese. Transfer the grits to a bowl and let them cool for just 10 to 15 minutes.

2. Stir the ham, chives and the rest of the cheese into the grits and season with salt and pepper to taste. Add the beaten egg and refrigerate the mixture for 30 minutes. (Try not to chill the grits much longer than 30 minutes, or the mixture will be too firm to shape into patties.)

3. While the grit mixture is chilling, make the country gravy and set it aside.

4. Place the panko breadcrumbs in a shallow dish. Measure out ¼-cup portions of the grits mixture and shape them into patties. Coat all sides of the patties with the panko breadcrumbs, patting them with your hands so the crumbs adhere to the patties. You should have about 16 patties. Spray both sides of the patties with oil.

5. Preheat the air fryer to 400°F.

6. In batches of 5 or 6, air-fry the fritters for 8 minutes. Using a flat spatula, flip the fritters over and air-fry for another 4 minutes.

7. Serve hot with country gravy.

Southwest Cornbread

Servings: 6
Cooking Time: 18 Minutes

Ingredients:

- cooking spray
- ½ cup yellow cornmeal
- ½ cup flour
- 2 teaspoons baking powder
- ½ teaspoon salt
- ½ cup frozen corn kernels, thawed and drained
- ¼ cup finely chopped onion
- 1 or 2 small jalapeño peppers, seeded and chopped
- 1 egg
- ½ cup milk
- 2 tablespoons melted butter
- 2 ounces sharp Cheddar cheese, grated

Directions:

1. Preheat air fryer to 360°F.
2. Spray air fryer baking pan with nonstick cooking spray.
3. In a medium bowl, stir together the cornmeal, flour, baking powder, and salt.
4. Stir in the corn, onion, and peppers.
5. In a small bowl, beat together the egg, milk, and butter. Stir into dry ingredients until well combined.
6. Spoon half the batter into prepared baking pan, spreading to edges. Top with grated cheese. Spoon remaining batter on top of cheese and gently spread to edges of pan so it completely covers the cheese.
7. Cook at 360°F for 18 minutes, until cornbread is done and top is crispy brown.

Fry Bread

Servings: 4
Cooking Time: 5 Minutes

Ingredients:

- 1 cup flour
- 2 teaspoons baking powder
- ¼ teaspoon salt
- ¼ cup lukewarm milk
- 1 teaspoon oil
- 2–3 tablespoons water
- oil for misting or cooking spray

Directions:

1. Stir together flour, baking powder, and salt. Gently mix in the milk and oil. Stir in 1 tablespoon water. If needed, add more water 1 tablespoon at a time until stiff dough forms. Dough shouldn't be sticky, so use only as much as you need.
2. Divide dough into 4 portions and shape into balls. Cover with a towel and let rest for 10minutes.
3. Preheat air fryer to 390°F.
4. Shape dough as desired:
5. a. Pat into 3-inch circles. This will make a thicker bread to eat plain or with a sprinkle of cinnamon or honey butter. You can cook all 4 at once.
6. b. Pat thinner into rectangles about 3 x 6 inches. This will create a thinner bread to serve as a base for dishes such as Indian tacos. The circular shape is more traditional, but rectangles allow you to cook 2 at a time in your air fryer basket.
7. Spray both sides of dough pieces with oil or cooking spray.
8. Place the 4 circles or 2 of the dough rectangles in the air fryer basket and cook at 390°F for 3minutes. Spray tops, turn, spray other side, and cook for 2 more minutes. If necessary, repeat to cook remaining bread.
9. Serve piping hot as is or allow to cool slightly and add toppings to create your own Native American tacos.

Cheddar-ham-corn Muffins

Servings: 8
Cooking Time: 8 Minutes

Ingredients:

- ¾ cup yellow cornmeal
- ¼ cup flour
- 1½ teaspoons baking powder
- ¼ teaspoon salt
- 1 egg, beaten
- 2 tablespoons canola oil
- ½ cup milk
- ½ cup shredded sharp Cheddar cheese
- ½ cup diced ham
- 8 foil muffin cups, liners removed and sprayed with cooking spray

Directions:

1. Preheat air fryer to 390°F.
2. In a medium bowl, stir together the cornmeal, flour, baking powder, and salt.
3. Add egg, oil, and milk to dry ingredients and mix well.
4. Stir in shredded cheese and diced ham.
5. Divide batter among the muffin cups.
6. Place 4 filled muffin cups in air fryer basket and bake for 5minutes.
7. Reduce temperature to 330°F and bake for 1 to 2minutes or until toothpick inserted in center of muffin comes out clean.
8. Repeat steps 6 and 7 to cook remaining muffins.

Sweet Potato-cinnamon Toast

Servings: 6

Cooking Time: 8 Minutes

Ingredients:

- 1 small sweet potato, cut into ⅜-inch slices
- oil for misting
- ground cinnamon

Directions:

1. Preheat air fryer to 390°F.
2. Spray both sides of sweet potato slices with oil. Sprinkle both sides with cinnamon to taste.
3. Place potato slices in air fryer basket in a single layer.
4. Cook for 4minutes, turn, and cook for 4 more minutes or until potato slices are barely fork tender.

Peppered Maple Bacon Knots

Servings: 6
Cooking Time: 8 Minutes

Ingredients:
- 1 pound maple smoked center-cut bacon
- ¼ cup maple syrup
- ¼ cup brown sugar
- coarsely cracked black peppercorns

Directions:
1. Tie each bacon strip in a loose knot and place them on a baking sheet.
2. Combine the maple syrup and brown sugar in a bowl. Brush each knot generously with this mixture and sprinkle with coarsely cracked black pepper.
3. Preheat the air fryer to 390°F.
4. Air-fry the bacon knots in batches. Place one layer of knots in the air fryer basket and air-fry for 5 minutes. Turn the bacon knots over and air-fry for an additional 3 minutes.
5. Serve warm.

Crustless Broccoli, Roasted Pepper And Fontina Quiche

Servings: 4

Cooking Time: 60 Minutes

Ingredients:

- 7-inch cake pan
- 1 cup broccoli florets
- ¾ cup chopped roasted red peppers
- 1¼ cups grated Fontina cheese
- 6 eggs
- ¾ cup heavy cream
- ½ teaspoon salt
- freshly ground black pepper

Directions:

1. Preheat the air fryer to 360°F.
2. Grease the inside of a 7-inch cake pan (4 inches deep) or other oven-safe pan that will fit into your air fryer. Place the broccoli florets and roasted red peppers in the cake pan and top with the grated Fontina cheese.
3. Whisk the eggs and heavy cream together in a bowl. Season the eggs with salt and freshly ground black pepper. Pour the egg mixture over the cheese and vegetables and cover the pan with aluminum foil. Transfer the cake pan to the air fryer basket.
4. Air-fry at 360°F for 60 minutes. Remove the aluminum foil for the last two minutes of cooking time.
5. Unmold the quiche onto a platter and cut it into slices to serve with a side salad or perhaps some air-fried potatoes.

VEGETABLE SIDE DISHES RECIPES

Bacon-wrapped Asparagus

Servings: 4
Cooking Time: 10 Minutes

Ingredients:
- 1 tablespoon extra-virgin olive oil
- ½ teaspoon sea salt
- ¼ cup grated Parmesan cheese
- 1 pound asparagus, ends trimmed
- 8 slices bacon

Directions:
1. Preheat the air fryer to 380°F.
2. In large bowl, mix together the olive oil, sea salt, and Parmesan cheese. Toss the asparagus in the olive oil mixture.
3. Evenly divide the asparagus into 8 bundles. Wrap 1 piece of bacon around each bundle, not overlapping the bacon but spreading it across the bundle.
4. Place the asparagus bundles into the air fryer basket, not touching. Work in batches as needed.
5. Cook for 8 minutes; check for doneness, and cook another 2 minutes.

Street Corn

Servings: 4
Cooking Time: 10 Minutes

Ingredients:
- 1 tablespoon butter
- 4 ears corn
- ⅓ cup plain Greek yogurt
- 2 tablespoons Parmesan cheese
- ½ teaspoon paprika
- ½ teaspoon garlic powder
- ¼ teaspoon salt
- ¼ teaspoon black pepper
- ¼ cup finely chopped cilantro

Directions:
1. Preheat the air fryer to 400°F.
2. In a medium microwave-safe bowl, melt the butter in the microwave. Lightly brush the outside of the ears of corn with the melted butter.
3. Place the corn into the air fryer basket and cook for 5 minutes, flip the corn, and cook another 5 minutes.
4. Meanwhile, in a medium bowl, mix the yogurt, cheese, paprika, garlic powder, salt, and pepper. Set aside.
5. Carefully remove the corn from the air fryer and let cool 3 minutes. Brush the outside edges with the yogurt mixture and top with fresh chopped cilantro. Serve immediately.

Roasted Eggplant Halves With Herbed Ricotta

Servings: 3

Cooking Time: 20 Minutes

Ingredients:

- 3 5- to 6-ounce small eggplants, stemmed
- Olive oil spray
- ¼ teaspoon Table salt
- ¼ teaspoon Ground black pepper
- ½ cup Regular or low-fat ricotta
- 1½ tablespoons Minced fresh basil leaves
- 1¼ teaspoons Minced fresh oregano leaves
- Honey

Directions:

1. Preheat the air fryer to 325°F (or 330°F, if that's the closest setting).
2. Cut the eggplants in half lengthwise. Set them cut side up on your work surface. Using the tip of a paring knife, make a series of slits about three-quarters down into the flesh of each eggplant half; work at a 45-degree angle to the (former) stem across the vegetable and make the slits about ½ inch apart. Make a second set of equidistant slits at a 90-degree angle to the first slits, thus creating a crosshatch pattern in the vegetable.
3. Generously coat the cut sides of the eggplants with olive oil spray. Sprinkle the salt and pepper over the cut surfaces.
4. Set the eggplant halves cut side up in the basket with as much air space between them as possible. Air-fry undisturbed for 20 minutes, or until soft and golden.
5. Use kitchen tongs to gently transfer the eggplant halves to serving plates or a platter. Cool for 5 minutes.
6. Whisk the ricotta, basil, and oregano in a small bowl until well combined. Top the eggplant halves with this mixture. Drizzle the halves with honey to taste before serving warm.

Moroccan-spiced Carrots

Servings: 4

Cooking Time: 30 Minutes

Ingredients:

- 1¼ pounds Baby carrots
- 2 tablespoons Butter, melted and cooled
- 1 teaspoon Mild smoked paprika
- 1 teaspoon Ground cumin
- ¾ teaspoon Ground coriander
- ¾ teaspoon Ground dried ginger
- ¼ teaspoon Ground cinnamon
- ½ teaspoon Table salt
- ¼ teaspoon Ground black pepper

Directions:

1. Preheat the air fryer to 400°F.
2. Toss the carrots, melted butter, smoked paprika, cumin, coriander, ginger, cinnamon, salt, and pepper in a large bowl until the carrots are evenly and thoroughly coated.
3. When the machine is at temperature, scrape the carrots into the basket, spreading them into as close to one layer as you can. Air-fry for 30 minutes, tossing and rearranging the carrots every 8 minutes (that is, three times), until crisp-tender and lightly browned in spots.
4. Pour the contents of the basket into a serving bowl or platter. Cool for a couple of minutes, then serve warm or at room temperature.

Panzanella Salad With Crispy Croutons

Servings: 4
Cooking Time: 3 Minutes

Ingredients:

- ½ French baguette, sliced in half lengthwise
- 2 large cloves garlic
- 2 large ripe tomatoes, divided
- 2 small Persian cucumbers, quartered and diced
- ¼ cup Kalamata olives
- 1 tablespoon chopped, fresh oregano or 1 teaspoon dried oregano
- ¼ cup chopped fresh basil
- ¼ cup chopped fresh parsley
- ½ cup sliced red onion
- 2 tablespoons red wine vinegar
- ¼ cup extra-virgin olive oil
- Salt and pepper, to taste

Directions:

1. Preheat the air fryer to 380°F.
2. Place the baguette into the air fryer and toast for 3 to 5 minutes or until lightly golden brown.
3. Remove the bread from air fryer and immediately rub 1 raw garlic clove firmly onto the inside portion of each piece of bread, scraping the garlic onto the bread.
4. Slice 1 of the tomatoes in half and rub the cut edge of one half of the tomato onto the toasted bread. Season the rubbed bread with sea salt to taste.
5. Cut the bread into cubes and place in a large bowl. Cube the remaining 1½ tomatoes and add to the bowl. Add the cucumbers, olives, oregano, basil, parsley, and onion; stir to mix. Drizzle the red wine vinegar into the bowl, and stir. Drizzle the olive oil over the top, stir, and adjust the seasonings with salt and pepper.
6. Serve immediately or allow to sit at room temperature up to 1 hour before serving.

Green Peas With Mint

Servings: 4

Cooking Time: 5 Minutes

Ingredients:

- 1 cup shredded lettuce
- 1 10-ounce package frozen green peas, thawed
- 1 tablespoon fresh mint, shredded
- 1 teaspoon melted butter

Directions:

1. Lay the shredded lettuce in the air fryer basket.
2. Toss together the peas, mint, and melted butter and spoon over the lettuce.
3. Cook at 360°F for 5minutes, until peas are warm and lettuce wilts.

Green Beans

Servings: 4
Cooking Time: 12 Minutes

Ingredients:

- 1 pound fresh green beans
- 2 tablespoons Italian salad dressing
- salt and pepper

Directions:

1. Wash beans and snap off stem ends.
2. In a large bowl, toss beans with Italian dressing.
3. Cook at 330°F for 5minutes. Shake basket or stir and cook 5minutes longer. Shake basket again and, if needed, continue cooking for 2 minutes, until as tender as you like. Beans should shrivel slightly and brown in places.
4. Sprinkle with salt and pepper to taste.

Steak Fries

Cooking Time: 20 Minutes
Servings: 4

Ingredients:
- 2 russet potatoes, scrubbed and cut into wedges lengthwise
- 1 tablespoon olive oil
- 2 teaspoons seasoning salt (recipe below)

Directions:
1. Preheat the air fryer to 400°F.
2. Toss the potatoes with the olive oil and the seasoning salt.
3. Air-fry for 20 minutes (depending on the size of the wedges), turning the potatoes over gently a few times throughout the cooking process to brown and cook them evenly.

Five-spice Roasted Sweet Potatoes

Servings: 4
Cooking Time: 12 Minutes

Ingredients:
- ½ teaspoon ground cinnamon
- ¼ teaspoon ground cumin
- ¼ teaspoon paprika
- 1 teaspoon chile powder
- ⅛ teaspoon turmeric
- ½ teaspoon salt (optional)
- freshly ground black pepper
- 2 large sweet potatoes, peeled and cut into ¾-inch cubes (about 3 cups)
- 1 tablespoon olive oil

Directions:
1. In a large bowl, mix together cinnamon, cumin, paprika, chile powder, turmeric, salt, and pepper to taste.
2. Add potatoes and stir well.
3. Drizzle the seasoned potatoes with the olive oil and stir until evenly coated.
4. Place seasoned potatoes in the air fryer baking pan or an ovenproof dish that fits inside your air fryer basket.
5. Cook for 6minutes at 390°F, stop, and stir well.
6. Cook for an additional 6minutes.

Stuffed Avocados

Servings: 4

Cooking Time: 8 Minutes

Ingredients:
- 1 cup frozen shoepeg corn, thawed
- 1 cup cooked black beans
- ¼ cup diced onion
- ½ teaspoon cumin
- 2 teaspoons lime juice, plus extra for serving
- salt and pepper
- 2 large avocados, split in half, pit removed

Directions:
1. Mix together the corn, beans, onion, cumin, and lime juice. Season to taste with salt and pepper.
2. Scoop out some of the flesh from center of each avocado and set aside. Divide corn mixture evenly between the cavities.
3. Set avocado halves in air fryer basket and cook at 360°F for 8 minutes, until corn mixture is hot.
4. Season the avocado flesh that you scooped out with a squirt of lime juice, salt, and pepper. Spoon it over the cooked halves.

BEEF , PORK & LAMB RECIPES

Steakhouse Burgers With Red Onion Compote

Servings: 4
Cooking Time: 22 Minutes

Ingredients:

- 1½ pounds lean ground beef
- 2 cloves garlic, minced and divided
- 1 teaspoon Worcestershire sauce
- 1 teaspoon sea salt, divided
- ½ teaspoon black pepper
- 1 tablespoon extra-virgin olive oil
- 1 red onion, thinly sliced
- ¼ cup balsamic vinegar
- 1 teaspoon sugar
- 1 tablespoon tomato paste
- 2 tablespoons mayonnaise
- 2 tablespoons sour cream
- 4 brioche hamburger buns
- 1 cup arugula

Directions:

1. In a large bowl, mix together the ground beef, 1 of the minced garlic cloves, the Worcestershire sauce, ½ teaspoon of the salt, and the black pepper. Form the meat into 1-inch-thick patties. Make a dent in the center (this helps the center cook evenly). Let the meat sit for 15 minutes.
2. Meanwhile, in a small saucepan over medium heat, cook the olive oil and red onion for 4 minutes, stirring frequently to avoid burning. Add in the balsamic vinegar, sugar, and tomato paste, and cook for an additional 3 minutes, stirring frequently. Transfer the onion compote to a small bowl.
3. Preheat the air fryer to 350°F.
4. In another small bowl, mix together the remaining minced garlic, the mayonnaise, and the sour cream. Spread the mayo mixture on the insides of the brioche buns.
5. Cook the hamburgers for 6 minutes, flip the burgers, and cook an additional 2 to 6 minutes. Check the internal temperature to avoid under- or overcooking. Hamburgers should be cooked to at least 160°F. After cooking, cover with foil and let the meat rest for 5 minutes.
6. Meanwhile, place the buns inside the air fryer and toast them for 3 minutes.
7. To assemble the burgers, place the hamburger on one side of the bun, top with onion compote and ¼ cup arugula, and then place the other half of the bun on top.

Perfect Strip Steaks

Servings: 2

Cooking Time: 17 Minutes

Ingredients:
- 1½ tablespoons Olive oil
- 1½ tablespoons Minced garlic
- 2 teaspoons Ground black pepper
- 1 teaspoon Table salt
- 2 ¾-pound boneless beef strip steak(s)

Directions:
1. Preheat the air fryer to 375°F (or 380°F or 390°F, if one of these is the closest setting).
2. Mix the oil, garlic, pepper, and salt in a small bowl, then smear this mixture over both sides of the steak(s).
3. When the machine is at temperature, put the steak(s) in the basket with as much air space as possible between them for the larger batch. They should not overlap or even touch. That said, even just a ¼-inch between them will work. Air-fry for 12 minutes, turning once, until an instant-read meat thermometer inserted into the thickest part of a steak registers 127°F for rare (not USDA-approved). Or air-fry for 15 minutes, turning once, until an instant-read meat thermometer registers 145°F for medium (USDA-approved). If the machine is at 390°F, the steaks may cook 2 minutes more quickly than the stated timing.
4. Use kitchen tongs to transfer the steak(s) to a wire rack. Cool for 5 minutes before serving.

Barbecue-style Beef Cube Steak

Servings: 2

Cooking Time: 14 Minutes

Ingredients:

- 2 4-ounce beef cube steak(s)
- 2 cups (about 8 ounces) Fritos (original flavor) or a generic corn chip equivalent, crushed to crumbs (see here)
- 6 tablespoons Purchased smooth barbecue sauce, any flavor (gluten-free, if a concern)

Directions:

1. Preheat the air fryer to 375°F .
2. Spread the Fritos crumbs in a shallow soup plate or a small pie plate. Rub the barbecue sauce onto both sides of the steak(s). Dredge the steak(s) in the Fritos crumbs to coat well and thoroughly, turning several times and pressing down to get the little bits to adhere to the meat.
3. When the machine is at temperature, set the steak(s) in the basket. Leave as much air space between them as possible if you're working with more than one piece of beef. Air-fry undisturbed for 12 minutes, or until lightly brown and crunchy. If the machine is at 360°F, you may need to add 2 minutes to the cooking time.
4. Use kitchen tongs to transfer the steak(s) to a wire rack. Cool for 5 minutes before serving.

Sweet And Sour Pork

Servings: 2
Cooking Time: 11 Minutes

Ingredients:

- ⅓ cup all-purpose flour
- ⅓ cup cornstarch
- 2 teaspoons Chinese 5-spice powder
- 1 teaspoon salt
- freshly ground black pepper
- 1 egg
- 2 tablespoons milk
- ¾ pound boneless pork, cut into 1-inch cubes
- vegetable or canola oil, in a spray bottle
- 1½ cups large chunks of red and green peppers
- ½ cup ketchup
- 2 tablespoons rice wine vinegar or apple cider vinegar
- 2 tablespoons brown sugar
- ¼ cup orange juice
- 1 tablespoon soy sauce
- 1 clove garlic, minced
- 1 cup cubed pineapple
- chopped scallions

Directions:

1. Set up a dredging station with two bowls. Combine the flour, cornstarch, Chinese 5-spice powder, salt and pepper in one large bowl. Whisk the egg and milk together in a second bowl. Dredge the pork cubes in the flour mixture first, then dip them into the egg and then back into the flour to coat on all sides. Spray the coated pork cubes with vegetable or canola oil.

2. Preheat the air fryer to 400°F.

3. Toss the pepper chunks with a little oil and air-fry at 400°F for 5 minutes, shaking the basket halfway through the cooking time.

4. While the peppers are cooking, start making the sauce. Combine the ketchup, rice wine vinegar, brown sugar, orange juice, soy sauce, and garlic in a medium saucepan and bring the mixture to a boil on the stovetop. Reduce the heat and simmer for 5 minutes. When the peppers have finished air-frying, add them to the saucepan along with the pineapple chunks. Simmer the peppers and pineapple in the sauce for an additional 2 minutes. Set aside and keep warm.

5. Add the dredged pork cubes to the air fryer basket and air-fry at 400°F for 6 minutes, shaking the basket to turn the cubes over for the last minute of the cooking process.

6. When ready to serve, toss the cooked pork with the pineapple, peppers and sauce. Serve over white rice and garnish with chopped scallions.

Meat Loaves

Servings: 4
Cooking Time: 19 Minutes

Ingredients:

- Sauce
- ¼ cup white vinegar
- ¼ cup brown sugar
- 2 tablespoons Worcestershire sauce
- ½ cup ketchup
- Meat Loaves
- 1 pound very lean ground beef
- ⅔ cup dry bread (approx. 1 slice torn into small pieces)
- 1 egg
- ⅓ cup minced onion
- 1 teaspoon salt
- 2 tablespoons ketchup

Directions:

1. In a small saucepan, combine all sauce ingredients and bring to a boil. Remove from heat and stir to ensure that brown sugar dissolves completely.
2. In a large bowl, combine the beef, bread, egg, onion, salt, and ketchup. Mix well.
3. Divide meat mixture into 4 portions and shape each into a thick, round patty. Patties will be about 3 to 3½ inches in diameter, and all four should fit easily into the air fryer basket at once.
4. Cook at 360°F for 18 minutes, until meat is well done. Baste tops of mini loaves with a small amount of sauce, and cook 1 minute.
5. Serve hot with additional sauce on the side.

Lamb Chops

Servings: 2
Cooking Time: 20 Minutes

Ingredients:

- 2 teaspoons oil
- ½ teaspoon ground rosemary
- ½ teaspoon lemon juice
- 1 pound lamb chops, approximately 1-inch thick
- salt and pepper
- cooking spray

Directions:

1. Mix the oil, rosemary, and lemon juice together and rub into all sides of the lamb chops. Season to taste with salt and pepper.
2. For best flavor, cover lamb chops and allow them to rest in the fridge for 20 minutes.
3. Spray air fryer basket with nonstick spray and place lamb chops in it.
4. Cook at 360°F for approximately 20minutes. This will cook chops to medium. The meat will be juicy but have no remaining pink. Cook for a minute or two longer for well done chops. For rare chops, stop cooking after about 12minutes and check for doneness.

Sausage-cheese Calzone

Servings: 8

Cooking Time: 8 Minutes

Ingredients:

- Crust
- 2 cups white wheat flour, plus more for kneading and rolling
- 1 package (¼ ounce) RapidRise yeast
- 1 teaspoon salt
- ½ teaspoon dried basil
- 1 cup warm water (115°F to 125°F)
- 2 teaspoons olive oil
- Filling
- ¼ pound Italian sausage
- ½ cup ricotta cheese
- 4 ounces mozzarella cheese, shredded
- ¼ cup grated Parmesan cheese
- oil for misting or cooking spray
- marinara sauce for serving

Directions:

1. Crumble Italian sausage into air fryer baking pan and cook at 390°F for 5minutes. Stir, breaking apart, and cook for 3 to 4minutes, until well done. Remove and set aside on paper towels to drain.

2. To make dough, combine flour, yeast, salt, and basil. Add warm water and oil and stir until a soft dough forms. Turn out onto lightly floured board and knead for 3 or 4minutes. Let dough rest for 10minutes.

3. To make filling, combine the three cheeses in a medium bowl and mix well. Stir in the cooked sausage.

4. Cut dough into 8 pieces.

5. Working with 4 pieces of the dough, press each into a circle about 5 inches in diameter. Top each dough circle with 2 heaping tablespoons of filling. Fold over to create a half-moon shape and press edges firmly together. Be sure that edges are firmly sealed to prevent leakage. Spray both sides with oil or cooking spray.

6. Place 4 calzones in air fryer basket and cook at 360°F for 5minutes. Mist with oil and cook for 3 minutes, until crust is done and nicely browned.

7. While the first batch is cooking, press out the remaining dough, fill, and shape into calzones.

8. Spray both sides with oil and cook for 5minutes. If needed, mist with oil and continue cooking for 3 minutes longer. This second batch will cook a little faster than the first because your air fryer is already hot.

9. Serve with marinara sauce on the side for dipping.

Crunchy Fried Pork Loin Chops

Servings: 3

Cooking Time: 12 Minutes

Ingredients:

- 1 cup All-purpose flour or tapioca flour
- 1 Large egg(s), well beaten
- 1½ cups Seasoned Italian-style dried bread crumbs (gluten-free, if a concern)
- 3 4- to 5-ounce boneless center-cut pork loin chops
- Vegetable oil spray

Directions:

1. Preheat the air fryer to 350°F .
2. Set up and fill three shallow soup plates or small pie plates on your counter: one for the flour, one for the beaten egg(s), and one for the bread crumbs.
3. Dredge a pork chop in the flour, coating both sides as well as around the edge. Gently shake off any excess, then dip the chop in the egg(s), again coating both sides and the edge. Let any excess egg slip back into the rest, then set the chop in the bread crumbs, turning it and pressing gently to coat well on both sides and the edge. Coat the pork chop all over with vegetable oil spray and set aside so you can dredge, coat, and spray the additional chop(s).
4. Set the chops in the basket with as much air space between them as possible. Air-fry undisturbed for 12 minutes, or until brown and crunchy and an instant-read meat thermometer inserted into the center of a chop registers 145°F.
5. Use kitchen tongs to transfer the chops to a wire rack. Cool for 5 minutes before serving.

Pork Schnitzel With Dill Sauce

Servings: 4

Cooking Time: 4 Minutes

Ingredients:

- 6 boneless, center cut pork chops (about 1½ pounds)
- ½ cup flour
- 1½ teaspoons salt
- freshly ground black pepper
- 2 eggs
- ½ cup milk
- 1½ cups toasted fine breadcrumbs
- 1 teaspoon paprika
- 3 tablespoons butter, melted
- 2 tablespoons vegetable or olive oil
- lemon wedges
- Dill Sauce:
- 1 cup chicken stock
- 1½ tablespoons cornstarch
- ⅓ cup sour cream
- 1½ tablespoons chopped fresh dill
- salt and pepper

Directions:

1. Trim the excess fat from the pork chops and pound each chop with a meat mallet between two pieces of plastic wrap until they are ½-inch thick.

2. Set up a dredging station. Combine the flour, salt, and black pepper in a shallow dish. Whisk the eggs and milk together in a second shallow dish. Finally, combine the breadcrumbs and paprika in a third shallow dish.

3. Dip each flattened pork chop in the flour. Shake off the excess flour and dip each chop into the egg mixture. Finally dip them into the breadcrumbs and press the breadcrumbs onto the meat firmly. Place each finished chop on a baking sheet until they are all coated.

4. Preheat the air fryer to 400°F.

5. Combine the melted butter and the oil in a small bowl and lightly brush both sides of the coated pork chops. Do not brush the chops too heavily or the breading will not be as crispy.

6. Air-fry one schnitzel at a time for 4 minutes, turning it over halfway through the cooking time. Hold the cooked schnitzels warm on a baking pan in a 170°F oven while you finish air-frying the rest.

7. While the schnitzels are cooking, whisk the chicken stock and cornstarch together in a small saucepan over medium-high heat on the stovetop. Bring the mixture to a boil and simmer for 2 minutes. Remove the saucepan from heat and whisk in the sour cream. Add the chopped fresh dill and season with salt and pepper.

8. Transfer the pork schnitzel to a platter and serve with dill sauce and lemon wedges. For a traditional meal, serve this along side some egg noodles, spätzle or German potato salad.

Chicken-fried Steak

Servings: 2
Cooking Time: 12 Minutes

Ingredients:
- 1½ cups All-purpose flour
- 2 Large egg(s)
- 2 tablespoons Regular or low-fat sour cream
- 2 tablespoons Worcestershire sauce
- 2 ¼-pound thin beef cube steak(s)
- Vegetable oil spray

Directions:
1. Preheat the air fryer to 400°F.
2. Set up and fill two shallow soup plates or small pie plates on your counter: one for the flour; and one for the egg(s), whisked with the sour cream and Worcestershire sauce until uniform.
3. Dredge a piece of beef in the flour, coating it well on both sides and even along the edge. Shake off any excess; then dip the meat in the egg mixture, coating both sides while retaining the flour on the meat. Let any excess egg mixture slip back into the rest. Dredge the meat in the flour once again, coating all surfaces well. Gently shake off the excess coating and set the steak aside if you're coating another steak or two. Once done, coat the steak(s) on both sides with the vegetable oil spray.
4. Set the steak(s) in the basket. If there's more than one steak, make sure they do not overlap or even touch, although the smallest gap between them is enough to get them crunchy. Air-fry undisturbed for 6 minutes.
5. Use kitchen tongs to pick up one of the steaks. Coat it again on both sides with vegetable oil spray. Turn it upside down and set it back in the basket with that same regard for the space between them in larger batches. Repeat with any other steaks. Continue air-frying undisturbed for 6 minutes, or until golden brown and crunchy.
6. Use kitchen tongs to transfer the steak(s) to a wire rack. Cool for 5 minutes before serving.\

APPETIZERS AND SNACKS

Cheese Straws

Servings: 8

Cooking Time: 7 Minutes

Ingredients:

- For dusting All-purpose flour
- Two quarters of one thawed sheet (that is, a half of the sheet cut into two even pieces; wrap and refreeze the remainder) A 17.25-ounce box frozen puff pastry
- 1 Large egg(s)
- 2 tablespoons Water
- ¼ cup (about ¾ ounce) Finely grated Parmesan cheese
- up to 1 teaspoon Ground black pepper

Directions:

1. Preheat the air fryer to 400°F.
2. Dust a clean, dry work surface with flour. Set one of the pieces of puff pastry on top, dust the pastry lightly with flour, and roll with a rolling pin to a 6-inch square.
3. Whisk the egg(s) and water in a small or medium bowl until uniform. Brush the pastry square(s) generously with this mixture. Sprinkle each square with 2 tablespoons grated cheese and up to ½ teaspoon ground black pepper.
4. Cut each square into 4 even strips. Grasp each end of 1 strip with clean, dry hands; twist it into a cheese straw. Place the twisted straws on a baking sheet.
5. Lay as many straws as will fit in the air-fryer basket—as a general rule, 4 of them in a small machine, 5 in a medium model, or 6 in a large. There should be space for air to circulate around the straws. Set the baking sheet with any remaining straws in the fridge.
6. Air-fry undisturbed for 7 minutes, or until puffed and crisp. Use tongs to transfer the cheese straws to a wire rack, then make subsequent batches in the same way (keeping the baking sheet with the remaining straws in the fridge as each batch cooks). Serve warm.

Zucchini Fries With Roasted Garlic Aïoli

Servings: 4

Cooking Time: 12 Minutes

Ingredients:

- Roasted Garlic Aïoli:
- 1 teaspoon roasted garlic
- ½ cup mayonnaise
- 2 tablespoons olive oil
- juice of ½ lemon
- salt and pepper
- Zucchini Fries:
- ½ cup flour
- 2 eggs, beaten
- 1 cup seasoned breadcrumbs
- salt and pepper
- 1 large zucchini, cut into ½-inch sticks
- olive oil in a spray bottle, can or mister

Directions:

1. To make the aïoli, combine the roasted garlic, mayonnaise, olive oil and lemon juice in a bowl and whisk well. Season the aïoli with salt and pepper to taste.
2. Prepare the zucchini fries. Create a dredging station with three shallow dishes. Place the flour in the first shallow dish and season well with salt and freshly ground black pepper. Put the beaten eggs in the second shallow dish. In the third shallow dish, combine the breadcrumbs, salt and pepper. Dredge the zucchini sticks, coating with flour first, then dipping them into the eggs to coat, and finally tossing in breadcrumbs. Shake the dish with the breadcrumbs and pat the crumbs onto the zucchini sticks gently with your hands so they stick evenly.
3. Place the zucchini fries on a flat surface and let them sit at least 10 minutes before air-frying to let them dry out a little. Preheat the air fryer to 400°F.
4. Spray the zucchini sticks with olive oil, and place them into the air fryer basket. You can air-fry the zucchini in two layers, placing the second layer in the opposite direction to the first. Air-fry for 12 minutes turning and rotating the fries halfway through the cooking time. Spray with additional oil when you turn them over.
5. Serve zucchini fries warm with the roasted garlic aïoli.

Spicy Sweet Potato Tater-tots

Servings: 6

Cooking Time: 10 Minutes

Ingredients:

- 6 cups filtered water
- 2 medium sweet potatoes, peeled and cut in half
- 1 teaspoon garlic powder
- ½ teaspoon black pepper, divided
- ½ teaspoon salt, divided
- 1 cup panko breadcrumbs
- 1 teaspoon blackened seasoning

Directions:

1. In a large stovetop pot, bring the water to a boil. Add the sweet potatoes and let boil about 10 minutes, until a metal fork prong can be inserted but the potatoes still have a slight give (not completely mashed).
2. Carefully remove the potatoes from the pot and let cool.
3. When you're able to touch them, grate the potatoes into a large bowl. Mix the garlic powder, ¼ teaspoon of the black pepper, and ¼ teaspoon of the salt into the potatoes. Place the mixture in the refrigerator and let set at least 45 minutes (if you're leaving them longer than 45 minutes, cover the bowl).
4. Before assembling, mix the breadcrumbs and blackened seasoning in a small bowl.
5. Remove the sweet potatoes from the refrigerator and preheat the air fryer to 400°F.
6. Assemble the tater-tots by using a teaspoon to portion batter evenly and form into a tater-tot shape. Roll each tater-tot in the breadcrumb mixture. Then carefully place the tater-tots in the air fryer basket. Be sure that you've liberally sprayed the air fryer basket with an olive oil mist. Repeat until tater-tots fill the basket without touching one another. You'll need to do multiple batches, depending on the size of your air fryer.
7. Cook the tater-tots for 3 to 6 minutes, flip, and cook another 3 to 6 minutes.
8. Remove from the air fryer carefully and keep warm until ready to serve.

Thick-crust Pepperoni Pizza

Servings: 2
Cooking Time: 10 Minutes

Ingredients:

- 10 ounces Purchased fresh pizza dough (not a prebaked crust)
- Olive oil spray
- ¼ cup Purchased pizza sauce
- 10 slices Sliced pepperoni
- ⅓ cup Purchased shredded Italian 3- or 4-cheese blend

Directions:

1. Preheat the air fryer to 400°F.
2. Generously coat the inside of a 6-inch round cake pan for a small air fryer, a 7-inch round cake pan for a medium air fryer, or an 8-inch round cake pan for a large model with olive oil spray.
3. Set the dough in the pan and press it to fill the bottom in an even, thick layer. Spread the sauce over the dough, then top with the pepperoni and cheese.
4. When the machine is at temperature, set the pan in the basket and air-fry undisturbed for 10 minutes, or until puffed, brown, and bubbling.
5. Use kitchen tongs to transfer the cake pan to a wire rack. Cool for only a minute or so. Use a spatula to loosen the pizza from the pan and lift it out and onto the rack. Continue cooling for a few minutes before cutting into wedges to serve.

Polenta Fries With Chili-lime Mayo

Servings: 4
Cooking Time: 28 Minutes

Ingredients:

- 2 teaspoons vegetable or olive oil
- ¼ teaspoon paprika
- 1 pound prepared polenta, cut into 3-inch x ½-inch sticks
- salt and freshly ground black pepper
- Chili-Lime Mayo
- ½ cup mayonnaise
- 1 teaspoon chili powder
- ¼ teaspoon ground cumin
- juice of half a lime
- 1 teaspoon chopped fresh cilantro
- salt and freshly ground black pepper

Directions:

1. Preheat the air fryer to 400°F.
2. Combine the oil and paprika and then carefully toss the polenta sticks in the mixture.
3. Air-fry the polenta fries at 400°F for 15 minutes. Gently shake the basket to rotate the fries and continue to air-fry for another 13 minutes or until the fries have browned nicely. Season to taste with salt and freshly ground black pepper.
4. To make the chili-lime mayo, combine all the ingredients in a small bowl and stir well.
5. Serve the polenta fries warm with chili-lime mayo on the side for dipping.

Herbed Cheese Brittle

Servings: 4
Cooking Time: 5 Minutes

Ingredients:

- ½ cup shredded Parmesan cheese
- ½ cup shredded white cheddar cheese
- 1 tablespoon fresh chopped rosemary
- 1 teaspoon garlic powder
- 1 large egg white

Directions:

1. Preheat the air fryer to 400°F.
2. In a large bowl, mix the cheeses, rosemary, and garlic powder. Mix in the egg white. Then pour the batter into a 7-inch pan (or an air-fryer-compatible pan). Place the pan in the air fryer basket and cook for 4 to 5 minutes, or until the cheese is melted and slightly browned.
3. Remove the pan from the air fryer, and let it cool for 2 minutes. Invert the pan before the cheese brittle completely cools but is semi-hardened to allow it to easily slide out of the pan.
4. Let the pan cool another 5 minutes. Break into pieces and serve.

Onion Puffs

Servings: 14
Cooking Time: 8 Minutes

Ingredients:
- Vegetable oil spray
- ¾ cup Chopped yellow or white onion
- ½ cup Seasoned Italian-style panko bread crumbs
- 4½ tablespoons All-purpose flour
- 4½ tablespoons Whole, low-fat, or fat-free milk
- 1½ tablespoons Yellow cornmeal
- 1¼ teaspoons Granulated white sugar
- ½ teaspoon Baking powder
- ¼ teaspoon Table salt

Directions:
1. Cut or tear a piece of aluminum foil so that it lines the air fryer's basket with a ½-inch space on each of its four sides. Lightly coat the foil with vegetable oil spray, then set the foil sprayed side up inside the basket.
2. Preheat the air fryer to 400°F.
3. Stir the onion, bread crumbs, flour, milk, cornmeal, sugar, baking powder, and salt in a bowl to form a thick batter.
4. Remove the basket from the machine. Drop the onion batter by 2-tablespoon measures onto the foil, spacing the mounds evenly across its surface. Return the basket to the machine and air-fry undisturbed for 4 minutes.
5. Remove the basket from the machine. Lightly coat the puffs with vegetable oil spray. Use kitchen tongs to pick up a corner of the foil, then gently pull it out of the basket, letting the puffs slip onto the basket directly. Return the basket to the machine and continue air-frying undisturbed for 8 minutes, or until brown and crunchy.
6. Use kitchen tongs to transfer the puffs to a wire rack or a serving platter. Cool for 5 minutes before serving.

Potato Chips

Servings: 2
Cooking Time: 15 Minutes

Ingredients:

- 2 medium potatoes
- 2 teaspoons extra-light olive oil
- oil for misting or cooking spray
- salt and pepper

Directions:

1. Peel the potatoes.
2. Using a mandoline or paring knife, shave potatoes into thin slices, dropping them into a bowl of water as you cut them.
3. Dry potatoes as thoroughly as possible with paper towels or a clean dish towel. Toss potato slices with the oil to coat completely.
4. Spray air fryer basket with cooking spray and add potato slices.
5. Stir and separate with a fork.
6. Cook 390°F for 5minutes. Stir and separate potato slices. Cook 5 more minutes. Stir and separate potatoes again. Cook another 5minutes.
7. Season to taste.

String Bean Fries

Servings: 4
Cooking Time: 6 Minutes

Ingredients:

- ½ pound fresh string beans
- 2 eggs
- 4 teaspoons water
- ½ cup white flour
- ½ cup breadcrumbs
- ¼ teaspoon salt
- ¼ teaspoon ground black pepper
- ¼ teaspoon dry mustard (optional)
- oil for misting or cooking spray

Directions:

1. Preheat air fryer to 360°F.
2. Trim stem ends from string beans, wash, and pat dry.
3. In a shallow dish, beat eggs and water together until well blended.
4. Place flour in a second shallow dish.
5. In a third shallow dish, stir together the breadcrumbs, salt, pepper, and dry mustard if using.
6. Dip each string bean in egg mixture, flour, egg mixture again, then breadcrumbs.
7. When you finish coating all the string beans, open air fryer and place them in basket.
8. Cook for 3minutes.
9. Stop and mist string beans with oil or cooking spray.
10. Cook for 3 moreminutes or until string beans are crispy and nicely browned.

Fried Olives

Servings: 5
Cooking Time: 10 Minutes

Ingredients:

- ⅓ cup All-purpose flour or tapioca flour
- 1 Large egg white(s)
- 1 tablespoon Brine from the olive jar
- ⅔ cup Plain dried bread crumbs (gluten-free, if a concern)
- 15 Large pimiento-stuffed green olives
- Olive oil spray

Directions:

1. Preheat the air fryer to 400°F.
2. Pour the flour in a medium-size zip-closed plastic bag. Whisk the egg white and pickle brine in a medium bowl until foamy. Spread out the bread crumbs on a dinner plate.
3. Pour all the olives into the bag with the flour, seal, and shake to coat the olives. Remove a couple of olives, shake off any excess flour, and drop them into the egg white mixture. Toss gently but well to coat. Pick them up one at a time and roll each in the bread crumbs until well coated on all sides, even the ends. Set them aside on a cutting board as you finish the rest. When done, coat the olives with olive oil spray on all sides.
4. Place the olives in the basket in one layer. Air-fry for 8 minutes, gently shaking the basket once halfway through the cooking process to rearrange the olives, until lightly browned.
5. Gently pour the olives onto a wire rack and cool for at least 10 minutes before serving. Once cooled, the olives may be stored in a sealed container in the fridge for up to 2 days. To rewarm them, set them in the basket of a heated 400°F air fryer undisturbed for 2 minutes.

POULTRY RECIPES

Chicken Parmesan

Servings: 4
Cooking Time: 11 Minutes

Ingredients:
- 4 chicken tenders
- Italian seasoning
- salt
- ¼ cup cornstarch
- ½ cup Italian salad dressing
- ¼ cup panko breadcrumbs
- ¼ cup grated Parmesan cheese, plus more for serving
- oil for misting or cooking spray
- 8 ounces spaghetti, cooked
- 1 24-ounce jar marinara sauce

Directions:
1. Pound chicken tenders with meat mallet or rolling pin until about ¼-inch thick.
2. Sprinkle both sides with Italian seasoning and salt to taste.
3. Place cornstarch and salad dressing in 2 separate shallow dishes.
4. In a third shallow dish, mix together the panko crumbs and Parmesan cheese.
5. Dip flattened chicken in cornstarch, then salad dressing. Dip in the panko mixture, pressing into the chicken so the coating sticks well.
6. Spray both sides with oil or cooking spray. Place in air fryer basket in single layer.
7. Cook at 390°F for 5minutes. Spray with oil again, turning chicken to coat both sides. See tip about turning.
8. Cook for an additional 6 minutes or until chicken juices run clear and outside is browned.
9. While chicken is cooking, heat marinara sauce and stir into cooked spaghetti.
10. To serve, divide spaghetti with sauce among 4 dinner plates, and top each with a fried chicken tender. Pass additional Parmesan at the table for those who want extra cheese.

Chicken Wellington

Servings: 2
Cooking Time: 31 Minutes

Ingredients:

- 2 (5-ounce) boneless, skinless chicken breasts
- ½ cup White Worcestershire sauce
- 3 tablespoons butter
- ½ cup finely diced onion (about ½ onion)
- 8 ounces button mushrooms, finely chopped
- ¼ cup chicken stock
- 2 tablespoons White Worcestershire sauce (or white wine)
- salt and freshly ground black pepper
- 1 tablespoon chopped fresh tarragon
- 2 sheets puff pastry, thawed
- 1 egg, beaten
- vegetable oil

Directions:

1. Place the chicken breasts in a shallow dish. Pour the White Worcestershire sauce over the chicken coating both sides and marinate for 30 minutes.

2. While the chicken is marinating, melt the butter in a large skillet over medium-high heat on the stovetop. Add the onion and sauté for a few minutes, until it starts to soften. Add the mushrooms and sauté for 5 minutes until the vegetables are brown and soft. Deglaze the skillet with the chicken stock, scraping up any bits from the bottom of the pan. Add the White Worcestershire sauce and simmer for 3 minutes until the mixture reduces and starts to thicken. Season with salt and freshly ground black pepper. Remove the mushroom mixture from the heat and stir in the fresh tarragon. Let the mushroom mixture cool.

3. Preheat the air fryer to 360°F.

4. Remove the chicken from the marinade and transfer it to the air fryer basket. Tuck the small end of the chicken breast under the thicker part to shape it into a circle rather than an oval. Pour the marinade over the chicken and air-fry for 10 minutes.

5. Roll out the puff pastry and cut out two 6-inch squares. Brush the perimeter of each square with the egg wash. Place half of the mushroom mixture in the center of each puff pastry square. Place the chicken breasts, top side down on the mushroom mixture. Starting with one corner of puff pastry and working in one direction, pull the pastry up over the chicken to enclose it and press the ends of the pastry together in the middle. Brush the pastry with the egg wash to seal the edges. Turn the Wellingtons over and set aside.

6. To make a decorative design with the remaining puff pastry, cut out four 10-inch strips. For each Wellington, twist two of the strips together, place them over the chicken breast wrapped in puff pastry, and tuck the ends underneath to seal it. Brush the entire top and sides of the Wellingtons with the egg wash.

7. Preheat the air fryer to 350°F.

8. Spray or brush the air fryer basket with vegetable oil. Air-fry the chicken Wellingtons for 13 minutes. Carefully turn the Wellingtons over. Air-fry for another 8 minutes. Transfer to serving plates, light a candle and enjoy!

Teriyaki Chicken Legs

Servings: 2
Cooking Time: 20 Minutes

Ingredients:

- 4 tablespoons teriyaki sauce
- 1 tablespoon orange juice
- 1 teaspoon smoked paprika
- 4 chicken legs
- cooking spray

Directions:

1. Mix together the teriyaki sauce, orange juice, and smoked paprika. Brush on all sides of chicken legs.
2. Spray air fryer basket with nonstick cooking spray and place chicken in basket.
3. Cook at 360°F for 6minutes. Turn and baste with sauce. Cook for 6 moreminutes, turn and baste. Cook for 8 minutes more, until juices run clear when chicken is pierced with a fork.

Simple Buttermilk Fried Chicken

Servings: 4

Cooking Time: 27 Minutes

Ingredients:

- 1 (4-pound) chicken, cut into 8 pieces
- 2 cups buttermilk
- hot sauce (optional)
- 1½ cups flour*
- 2 teaspoons paprika
- 1 teaspoon salt
- freshly ground black pepper
- 2 eggs, lightly beaten
- vegetable oil, in a spray bottle

Directions:

1. Cut the chicken into 8 pieces and submerge them in the buttermilk and hot sauce, if using. A zipper-sealable plastic bag works well for this. Let the chicken soak in the buttermilk for at least one hour or even overnight in the refrigerator.

2. Set up a dredging station. Mix the flour, paprika, salt and black pepper in a clean zipper-sealable plastic bag. Whisk the eggs and place them in a shallow dish. Remove four pieces of chicken from the buttermilk and transfer them to the bag with the flour. Shake them around to coat on all sides. Remove the chicken from the flour, shaking off any excess flour, and dip them into the beaten egg. Return the chicken to the bag of seasoned flour and shake again. Set the coated chicken aside and repeat with the remaining four pieces of chicken.

3. Preheat the air fryer to 370°F.

4. Spray the chicken on all sides with the vegetable oil and then transfer one batch to the air fryer basket. Air-fry the chicken at 370°F for 20 minutes, flipping the pieces over halfway through the cooking process, taking care not to knock off the breading. Transfer the chicken to a plate, but do not cover. Repeat with the second batch of chicken.

5. Lower the temperature on the air fryer to 340°F. Flip the chicken back over and place the first batch of chicken on top of the second batch already in the basket. Air-fry for another 7 minutes and serve warm.

Fiesta Chicken Plate

Servings: 4
Cooking Time: 15 Minutes

Ingredients:

- 1 pound boneless, skinless chicken breasts (2 large breasts)
- 2 tablespoons lime juice
- 1 teaspoon cumin
- ½ teaspoon salt
- ½ cup grated Pepper Jack cheese
- 1 16-ounce can refried beans
- ½ cup salsa
- 2 cups shredded lettuce
- 1 medium tomato, chopped
- 2 avocados, peeled and sliced
- 1 small onion, sliced into thin rings
- sour cream
- tortilla chips (optional)

Directions:

1. Split each chicken breast in half lengthwise.
2. Mix lime juice, cumin, and salt together and brush on all surfaces of chicken breasts.
3. Place in air fryer basket and cook at 390°F for 15 minutes, until well done.
4. Divide the cheese evenly over chicken breasts and cook for an additional minute to melt cheese.
5. While chicken is cooking, heat refried beans on stovetop or in microwave.
6. When ready to serve, divide beans among 4 plates. Place chicken breasts on top of beans and spoon salsa over. Arrange the lettuce, tomatoes, and avocados artfully on each plate and scatter with the onion rings.
7. Pass sour cream at the table and serve with tortilla chips if desired.

Air-fried Turkey Breast With Cherry Glaze

Servings: 6
Cooking Time: 54 Minutes

Ingredients:

- 1 (5-pound) turkey breast
- 2 teaspoons olive oil
- 1 teaspoon dried thyme
- ½ teaspoon dried sage
- 1 teaspoon salt
- ½ teaspoon freshly ground black pepper
- ½ cup cherry preserves
- 1 tablespoon chopped fresh thyme leaves
- 1 teaspoon soy sauce*
- freshly ground black pepper

Directions:

1. All turkeys are built differently, so depending on the turkey breast and how your butcher has prepared it, you may need to trim the bottom of the ribs in order to get the turkey to sit upright in the air fryer basket without touching the heating element. The key to this recipe is getting the right size turkey breast. Once you've managed that, the rest is easy, so make sure your turkey breast fits into the air fryer basket before you Preheat the air fryer.
2. Preheat the air fryer to 350°F.
3. Brush the turkey breast all over with the olive oil. Combine the thyme, sage, salt and pepper and rub the outside of the turkey breast with the spice mixture.
4. Transfer the seasoned turkey breast to the air fryer basket, breast side up, and air-fry at 350°F for 25 minutes. Turn the turkey breast on its side and air-fry for another 12 minutes. Turn the turkey breast on the opposite side and air-fry for 12 more minutes. The internal temperature of the turkey breast should reach 165°F when fully cooked.
5. While the turkey is air-frying, make the glaze by combining the cherry preserves, fresh thyme, soy sauce and pepper in a small bowl. When the cooking time is up, return the turkey breast to an upright position and brush the glaze all over the turkey. Air-fry for a final 5 minutes, until the skin is nicely browned and crispy. Let the turkey rest, loosely tented with foil, for at least 5 minutes before slicing and serving.

Sesame Orange Chicken

Servings: 2
Cooking Time: 9 Minutes

Ingredients:

- 1 pound boneless, skinless chicken breasts, cut into cubes
- salt and freshly ground black pepper
- ¼ cup cornstarch
- 2 eggs, beaten
- 1½ cups panko breadcrumbs
- vegetable or peanut oil, in a spray bottle
- 12 ounces orange marmalade
- 1 tablespoon soy sauce
- 1 teaspoon minced ginger
- 2 tablespoons hoisin sauce
- 1 tablespoon sesame oil
- sesame seeds, toasted

Directions:

1. Season the chicken pieces with salt and pepper. Set up a dredging station. Put the cornstarch in a zipper-sealable plastic bag. Place the beaten eggs in a bowl and put the panko breadcrumbs in a shallow dish. Transfer the seasoned chicken to the bag with the cornstarch and shake well to completely coat the chicken on all sides. Remove the chicken from the bag, shaking off any excess cornstarch and dip the pieces into the egg. Let any excess egg drip from the chicken and transfer into the breadcrumbs, pressing the crumbs onto the chicken pieces with your hands. Spray the chicken pieces with vegetable or peanut oil.
2. Preheat the air fryer to 400°F.
3. Combine the orange marmalade, soy sauce, ginger, hoisin sauce and sesame oil in a saucepan. Bring the mixture to a boil on the stovetop, lower the heat and simmer for 10 minutes, until the sauce has thickened. Set aside and keep warm.
4. Transfer the coated chicken to the air fryer basket and air-fry at 400°F for 9 minutes, shaking the basket a few times during the cooking process to help the chicken cook evenly.
5. Right before serving, toss the browned chicken pieces with the sesame orange sauce. Serve over white rice with steamed broccoli. Sprinkle the sesame seeds on top.

Crispy "fried" Chicken

Servings: 4
Cooking Time: 14 Minutes

Ingredients:
- ¾ cup all-purpose flour
- ½ teaspoon paprika
- ¼ teaspoon black pepper
- ¼ teaspoon salt
- 2 large eggs
- 1½ cups panko breadcrumbs
- 1 pound boneless, skinless chicken tenders

Directions:
1. Preheat the air fryer to 400°F.
2. In a shallow bowl, mix the flour with the paprika, pepper, and salt.
3. In a separate bowl, whisk the eggs; set aside.
4. In a third bowl, place the breadcrumbs.
5. Liberally spray the air fryer basket with olive oil spray.
6. Pat the chicken tenders dry with a paper towel. Dredge the tenders one at a time in the flour, then dip them in the egg, and toss them in the breadcrumb coating. Repeat until all tenders are coated.
7. Set each tender in the air fryer, leaving room on each side of the tender to allow for flipping.
8. When the basket is full, cook 4 to 7 minutes, flip, and cook another 4 to 7 minutes.
9. Remove the tenders and let cool 5 minutes before serving. Repeat until all tenders are cooked.

Southern-fried Chicken Livers

Servings: 4
Cooking Time: 12 Minutes

Ingredients:

- 2 eggs
- 2 tablespoons water
- ¾ cup flour
- 1½ cups panko breadcrumbs
- ½ cup plain breadcrumbs
- 1 teaspoon salt
- ½ teaspoon black pepper
- 20 ounces chicken livers, salted to taste
- oil for misting or cooking spray

Directions:

1. Beat together eggs and water in a shallow dish. Place the flour in a separate shallow dish.
2. In the bowl of a food processor, combine the panko, plain breadcrumbs, salt, and pepper. Process until well mixed and panko crumbs are finely crushed. Place crumbs in a third shallow dish.
3. Dip livers in flour, then egg wash, and then roll in panko mixture to coat well with crumbs.
4. Spray both sides of livers with oil or cooking spray. Cooking in two batches, place livers in air fryer basket in single layer.
5. Cook at 390°F for 7minutes. Spray livers, turn over, and spray again. Cook for 5 more minutes, until done inside and coating is golden brown.
6. Repeat to cook remaining livers.

Spicy Black Bean Turkey Burgers With Cumin-avocado Spread

Servings: 2

Cooking Time: 20 Minutes

Ingredients:

- 1 cup canned black beans, drained and rinsed
- ¾ pound lean ground turkey
- 2 tablespoons minced red onion
- 1 Jalapeño pepper, seeded and minced
- 2 tablespoons plain breadcrumbs
- ½ teaspoon chili powder
- ¼ teaspoon cayenne pepper
- salt, to taste
- olive or vegetable oil
- 2 slices pepper jack cheese
- toasted burger rolls, sliced tomatoes, lettuce leaves
- Cumin-Avocado Spread:
- 1 ripe avocado
- juice of 1 lime
- 1 teaspoon ground cumin
- ½ teaspoon salt
- 1 tablespoon chopped fresh cilantro
- freshly ground black pepper

Directions:

1. Place the black beans in a large bowl and smash them slightly with the back of a fork. Add the ground turkey, red onion, Jalapeño pepper, breadcrumbs, chili powder and cayenne pepper. Season with salt. Mix with your hands to combine all the ingredients and then shape them into 2 patties. Brush both sides of the burger patties with a little olive or vegetable oil.

2. Preheat the air fryer to 380°F.

3. Transfer the burgers to the air fryer basket and air-fry for 20 minutes, flipping them over halfway through the cooking process. Top the burgers with the pepper jack cheese (securing the slices to the burgers with a toothpick) for the last 2 minutes of the cooking process.

4. While the burgers are cooking, make the cumin avocado spread. Place the avocado, lime juice, cumin and salt in food processor and process until smooth. (For a chunkier spread, you can mash this by hand in a bowl.) Stir in the cilantro and season with freshly ground black pepper. Chill the spread until you are ready to serve.

5. When the burgers have finished cooking, remove them from the air fryer and let them rest on a plate, covered gently with aluminum foil. Brush a little olive oil on the insides of the burger rolls. Place the rolls, cut side up, into the air fryer basket and air-fry at 400°F for 1 minute to toast and warm them.

6. Spread the cumin-avocado spread on the rolls and build your burgers with lettuce and sliced tomatoes and any other ingredient you like. Serve warm with a side of sweet potato fries.

RECIPES INDEX

A

Air-fried Turkey Breast With Cherry Glaze 104

Asian Glazed Meatballs 24

B

Bacon Puff Pastry Pinwheels 57

Bacon-wrapped Asparagus 65

Barbecue-style Beef Cube Steak 77

Blueberry Crisp 47

Blueberry Muffins 56

Broccoli Cheddar Stuffed Potatoes 38

C

Catfish Nuggets 15

Charred Cauliflower Tacos 31

Cheddar-ham-corn Muffins 61

Cheese Ravioli 35

Cheese Straws 88

Chicken Club Sandwiches 22

Chicken Gyros 21

Chicken Parmesan 98

Chicken Saltimbocca Sandwiches 27

Chicken Spiedies 23

Chicken Wellington 99

Chicken-fried Steak 87

Chocolate Macaroons 43

Coconut Crusted Bananas With Pineapple Sauce 45

Coconut Jerk Shrimp 18

Coconut-custard Pie 51

Crispy "fried" Chicken 106

Crispy Smelts 11

Crunchy Fried Pork Loin Chops 84

Crustless Broccoli, Roasted Pepper And Fontina Quiche 64

E

Easy Churros 49

Egg And Sausage Crescent Rolls 55

Egg Rolls 32

F

Falafel 36

Fiesta Chicken Plate 103

Fish Sticks For Kids 10

Fish Sticks With Tartar Sauce 14

Fish-in-chips 19

Five-spice Roasted Sweet Potatoes 73

Fried Cannoli Wontons 52

Fried Olives 97

Fried Snickers Bars 48

Fry Bread 60

Fudgy Brownie Cake 44

G

Giant Oatmeal–peanut Butter Cookie 50

Green Beans 71

Green Peas With Mint 70

H

Ham And Cheddar Gritters 58

Herbed Cheese Brittle 93

L

Lamb Chops 81

Lemon-dill Salmon Burgers 12

M

Meat Loaves 80

Mexican Twice Air-fried Sweet Potatoes 42

Mixed Berry Hand Pies 46

Moroccan-spiced Carrots 68

N

Nutella® Torte 53

Nutty Shrimp With Amaretto Glaze 17

O

Onion Puffs 94

P

Panzanella Salad With Crispy Croutons 69

Parmesan Portobello Mushroom Caps 39

Peppered Maple Bacon Knots 63

Perfect Strip Steaks 76

Polenta Fries With Chili-lime Mayo 92

Pork Schnitzel With Dill Sauce 85

Potato Chips 95

Potato-wrapped Salmon Fillets 16

Q

Quinoa Burgers With Feta Cheese And Dill 33

R

Reuben Sandwiches 25

Roasted Eggplant Halves With Herbed Ricotta 67

S

Salmon Burgers 28

Sausage And Pepper Heros 20

Sausage-cheese Calzone 82

Sesame Orange Chicken 105

Shrimp 13

Simple Buttermilk Fried Chicken 102

Southern-fried Chicken Livers 107

Southwest Cornbread 59

Spicy Black Bean Turkey Burgers With Cumin-avocado Spread 108

Spicy Sweet Potato Tater-tots 90

Spinach And Artichoke White Pizza 54

Steak Fries 72

Steakhouse Burgers With Red Onion Compote 75

Street Corn 66

String Bean Fries 96

Stuffed Avocados 74

Sweet And Sour Pork 78

Sweet Potato-cinnamon Toast 62

T

Tacos 40

Teriyaki Chicken Legs 101

Thai-style Pork Sliders 30

Thick-crust Pepperoni Pizza 91

Turkey Burgers 29

V

Vegetable Hand Pies 41

W

White Bean Veggie Burgers 26

Z

Zucchini Fries With Roasted Garlic Aïoli 89

CPSIA information can be obtained
at www.ICGtesting.com
Printed in the USA
BVHW090046060822
643962BV00005B/120